Taunton's

Kitchen

IDEA BOOK

Taunton's

Kitchen
IDEA BOOK

JOANNE KELLAR BOUKNIGHT

The Taunton Press

introduction

'M ALWAYS TUNED IN TO THE
shortcomings of kitchens, and I've had
lots more practice since our sons have
been living away from home. Our youngest
lives in a farmhouse at his Minnesota college
with 16 others. They cook dinners in a 12-ft.
by 12-ft. kitchen, then dine outdoors or in the
living room, plates on knees. The good cheer
and camaraderie are enviable, even if countertops are scarce and the range is tempera-
mental. Our oldest is a veteran of two Chicago
kitchenettes, but he figures a work triangle
that's actually just a short, straight line is
efficient, and it's easy enough to dine while
standing, saucepan in hand.

I'm guessing that you, too, have made
dinner in kitchens that look nothing like the
kitchens shown on these pages, and it's
possible your present-day kitchen is one of
those. That may be why you picked up this
book, because you spend time in a kitchen
that isn't really a dream come true.

First, you have to get started with your
kitchen design, and that can be a little scary.
One way to jump-start kitchen planning is by
making a playbook based on the kitchen
habits you have now. Go through the motions
of how you make dinner, or make a real dinner
while a family member makes notes on paper.
Observe how you make coffee, lunch, and
weekend meals. How do foods get washed,
cooked, served, and how does cleanup start?
How do you handle garbage and recycling
from the start of meal preparation to cleanup?

What else goes on in the kitchen besides
making, eating, and cleaning up food? Who
inhabits the kitchen throughout the day,
and how do they move through the kitchen
(whether or not they should). Study where
conflicts arise. Unless frequent entertaining
is a high priority, plan your kitchen design
around the average day, then incorporate
less frequent cooking activities. Write down
everything you would like in your dream

kitchen, from grand to small, from knocking out a wall to adding a single task light over a dark countertop corner.

As you shop for your dream kitchen, consider these economical options: shop online for bargains and one-of-a-kind sales, and check showrooms for discounted floor models. Shop in January for markdowns on appliances—and just about everything—as new models will be coming out soon and companies want to lower inventory. Find a contractor who may be tearing out an old kitchen, tour salvage companies, and check online for used kitchen elements. Be prepared to store any items that you are acquiring way ahead of schedule.

But don't forget to take a deep breath, especially if you've just moved into a house that has a college-student configuration. Take time to get to know the existing kitchen so that you know better what you want to keep, what to upgrade, and how things change over the course of a year. You may find you can live with less, and you'll definitely know where you'd like your morning coffee.

As you make decisions, balance style with function. While style can bring instant joy, function can bring long-term contentment. You don't need to choose the most durable kitchen elements if you are concerned that kitchen fashions will change, or if your budget can't handle the expense. Instead, choose a countertop like plastic laminate that you won't mind replacing after 10 years rather than an eons-worthy granite. On the other hand, if there's an expensive but gorgeous countertop that you will love in sickness and in health, and it won't break the bank, then go with your gut and get that countertop. Finally, be aware that buyer's remorse is a big part of new-kitchen planning. You will make decisions, and you will second-guess them. A few months after the kitchen is finished, you'll wonder what all the fuss was about.

start with layout and style

● ● ●

THE KITCHEN DEMANDS ATTENTION. NOT ONLY DOES IT COMMAND more money per square foot than any other room in the house but it's the room where everything happens, from the daily grind of coffee making to the once-a-year-blowout of Thanksgiving dinner. And that's why the kitchen is so exciting and challenging to plan and build. To make the job less overwhelming, keep in mind that your kitchen redo is for you and your family, not for some statistically average family. Don't be swept up with the latest kitchen fashions, unless they suit you and your dreams. Do consider kitchen trends such as energy efficiency and trimming square footage if you want to save money over the long haul. Look at what styles make you happy and combine them to your heart's content.

How your kitchen looks is a big deal, but how it works is even more important. A logical kitchen layout with easy-to-reach tools and well-placed equipment can make the ups and downs of daily life run so much smoother. Consider how the kitchen fits into the house. It's possible that opening up your existing kitchen to living spaces will revitalize not only the kitchen but the whole house.

Go ahead and choose that unusual backsplash that appeals to your soul (and satisfies your budget) or make the kitchen island taller than usual to suit your family of basketball players. Finally, take heart if you are in the market for a kitchen refresh rather than a redo; almost any change—as simple as paint or as expensive as replacing appliances—can transform not only the look of a kitchen but how well it works for you.

An inspired remodel of a 1970s redo took this kitchen back to its 1920s Mediterranean roots. Lots of interior storage keeps this sink wall free of cabinets. Locally made ceramic tiles imitate the brick exterior. The slab countertop is local walnut; the flooring is encaustic cement tile.

what's your ideal kitchen style?

● ● ● HOW DO YOU ENVISION YOUR IDEAL kitchen? Do you imagine rich, natural wood cabinets with frame-and-panel doors, or do you picture crisp, white subway tile? Or both? Chances are you've got a style image in mind. Unless you're aiming for museum-grade precision, you don't need to adhere to a textbook style from floor to ceiling. Instead, seek qualities that identify a particular style, such as the warmth, simplicity, and sense of comfort that a country-style kitchen radiates or the sophistication and serenity that a contemporary kitchen can convey. Whatever the style flavor you choose, if you employ it with a light touch you'll find it easier to refresh when it's time for an upgrade.

ABOVE A bright kitchen in a renovated 1920s Austin, TX, house feels both traditional and contemporary. The mosaic tiled countertop, flat aqua tile backsplash, and frame-and-panel doors are a blast from the past, while bar stools and shiny appliances add a modern polish.

ABOVE Stools with peeled-branch legs and an abundance of naturally finished wood give this country house a traditional rustic style. The running-bond rectangular tile backsplash offers a miniature version of the tile floor pattern.

FACING PAGE White is all over this serene contemporary kitchen, from composite countertop to cabinetry, and that's what allows color to pop, such as the gray veining in the marble backsplash and the richly stained wood bar stools.

RIGHT Furniture-like cabinet legs, open shelves supported by wood cleats and curved wood brackets, a profiled countertop, and frame-and-panel partial-overlay doors put this kitchen squarely in the traditional country style.

RIGHT Traditional custom cabinets pair with white subway tiles in this elegant kitchen. The white vertical surfaces are balanced by the dark horizontal surfaces of honed Absolute Black granite and red oak butcher-block countertops, walnut-stained floor, and taupe ceiling.

set the style...
WITH ONE KITCHEN ELEMENT, THEN GO FROM THERE

ust about every decision you make about kitchen design has an impact on another decision, but there's no rule that says to start with one particular decision first. If you find one element that really appeals to you, let it be your style springboard for the rest of the kitchen. You can choose colors, details, and materials that either complement or contrast your primary element. For example, if there's a particular slab of stone that you've fallen in love with (and it's within your budget), make it your kitchen design cornerstone and select cabinets, flooring, and countertop/backsplash materials to suit.

Or start with cabinets, which are prime purveyors of a kitchen's style. Once you've selected the cabinets, let their color and detailing inform the rest of your kitchen decisions. Even the tiniest of details, such as knobs and pulls, can flow from that first style decision. Just keep in mind that it's critical to make design decisions when your designer and/or contractor requests them so you don't hold up the job.

BELOW Contemporary cabinets with flat-slab doors and slender thumb pulls provide a streamlined contrast to the rough ceramic-tile backsplash. The rich Tuscan red unifies the two elements.

LEFT This Minnesota kitchen takes its style influence from traditional Scandinavian home design, with clean lines and light, cheery colors. The cabinets and butcher-block countertop are from IKEA®, and the floor is maple.

•trend watching

Trends are interesting to track, but jump on a trend bandwagon only if it's heading where you want to go. Trends that are fashion based—on a fabulous movie kitchen or on color forecasts—make sense only if they fit your sensibility and if you are comfortable with the fact that styles change. Cabinet materials vary in popularity over the years, but slowly. Cherry has been a perennial favorite for cabinets, and it still tops the charts according to the National Kitchen & Bath Association[SM] (NKBA), but maple remains popular, and walnut, oak, and bamboo are seeing more use, along with birch. The NKBA says stains are trending medium or dark, with light stains less popular. White remains the most popular paint color for cabinets. For walls, neutral paint colors such as gray, browns, white, and taupe are in style. Some fashion trends can change how kitchen space is shaped, such as swapping wall cabinets for either open shelves or a great view.

FACING PAGE, TOP A perfect blend of traditional and contemporary give this kitchen a warm and elegant style all its own. Stainless-steel countertops at the workspaces contrast with the range-side soapstone countertop and shiny marble backsplash. Custom cabinets have painted poplar frames and inset walnut doors and drawer faces. Modern-edged molding crowns the cabinets.

FACING PAGE, BOTTOM Contemporary in materials, detailing, and layout, this new kitchen is open to the dining/living spaces and is home to a well-used workspace (left).

ABOVE This renovated-down-to-the-studs kitchen received a traditional facelift with an antique range and face-frame cabinets with frame-and-panel doors and beadboard interiors. A pendant light fixture and bent plywood chairs add modern spice.

Traditional from furniture feet to crown-molded top, this cabinetry sports face-frame cases, inset frame-and-panel doors, butt hinges, and cupboard catches. Simple slab drawer fronts keep cabinets unfussy.

Function-based trends can have a big effect on style but most are more than skin deep. The following are some practical kitchen extras that many people crave these days: a pantry, open shelving, customized cabinet accessories, faucets with pull-out sprayers, dedicated space for recycling, a place to charge electronics, a place to work on computers, drinking-water filtration systems, and a flat-screen television.

Trends that are always worth following are increased energy efficiency, making kitchens smaller but smarter, choosing renewable materials and healthful finishes, and creating a stronger connection between the kitchen and the rest of the house—and to the outdoors.

ABOVE A blend of contemporary and traditional, this remodeled kitchen once had a single small window. That window has been enlarged, dropping to countertop level, and one entire wall of cabinetry was replaced with glass doors.

RIGHT There's no need for a view of the outdoors with a flat-screen television over the sink, but the window to the left offers a respite from the news. This location calls for a careful hand with the sprayer, though.

more about...
RESALE

t he average kitchen sees some kind of makeover every 15 years, often with a more complete overhaul during a strong economy and a lighter touch when money is tight. If you don't plan to be in your kitchen that long and plan to resell your home in the next few years, you may be concerned about what kind of kitchen will sell. National trends aren't as important as what sells in your neighborhood, so consult a local realtor to find out what is selling in the area.

style favorites

● ● ● TRADITIONAL STYLES HAVE LONG BEEN the preferred styles for new and renovated kitchens. Whatever you call a particular traditional style—country, rustic, Craftsman, French provincial, or Shaker, to name a few—its details and proportions are drawn from past eras, whether such details were actually used in kitchens themselves. In today's traditional-style kitchen, doors are likely to be frame-and-panel, possibly with beading. Panels can be flat, beveled, or glass of various textures. Modern/contemporary kitchens have been growing in popularity recently, with their streamlined flat-panel cabinetry, smooth backsplashes, and flat blocks of color, or minimal color. But according to the NKBA, transitional kitchens—kitchens with both contemporary and traditional aesthetics—are currently in vogue. That's because people aren't afraid to mix and match. Transitional kitchens tend to be subdued and classic in color but sparing in detail. *Eclectic* is another term for a mix of styles but is often reserved for kitchens that are designed as deliberate mash-ups of style, material, or color.

It made sense in this narrow townhouse to flatten the kitchen along one wall and open it up to the family room. In a way, this design hearkens back to the Colonial keeping room, where everything happened in one area. New skylights brighten the formerly dark space.

ABOVE Glass mosaic tiles top the backsplash popularity charts in part because of their jewel-like glow and wide array of rich colors. These golden yellow glass tiles are a sunny complement to slate gray cabinets and stainless-steel cooktop and shelf.

more about...
THE COST OF STYLE

t's tempting to think certain styles are more expensive than others. Modern design must be less expensive because there's less going on, right? But those crisp edges and perfectly flush surfaces take time and precision to achieve. In most cases, trimming a joint requires more material but is less labor intensive than finishing the joint itself. Of course, trim is available in a variety of profiles and materials, so it makes sense to choose those that suit your budget. Similarly, a smooth ceiling is ideal, but a textured surface doesn't require quite as fine a drywall finish, so it costs less.

ABOVE A sleek kitchen with glass backsplash and almost invisible cooktop (with hidden hood) contrasts with the polished wood. Cabinetry hides a wealth of storage, from flip-down spice racks to a toe-space step to make it easier to reach top cabinets.

LEFT This elegant but cozy room was designed in the unfitted kitchen style, which takes inspiration from traditional furniture, with varied cabinetry heights and depths and changes in countertop elevations and materials.

The style favorites of contemporary detailing and contrasting light and dark are in evidence in this urban kitchen redo. Streamlined frameless cabinets are mahogany, and countertops and backsplash are marble. Bold, angular cabinet pulls, sleek light fixtures, and an elegant faucet add to the modern polish.

quick fixes...
FOR STYLE

If budget and time constraints don't allow for big kitchen changes, small style fixes can solve some of your tired-kitchen woes. New cabinet hardware can freshen cabinets, as can the more labor- and time-intensive task of repainting doors, drawer faces, and cabinet interiors. Fresh paint can do wonders more quickly on walls and trim. Tile over a drywall backsplash if there's enough depth for the extra thickness. And go deeper than surface treatments to change not only style but convenience. Replace a flush-mounted light fixture with a period chandelier for instant glamour and more light on an island, or install LED or fluorescent surface-mounted lights under wall cabinets to brighten countertops. Change out appliances without changing their location for an update in not only style but function because new appliances will be more energy efficient and have more bells and whistles.

ABOVE White and stainless steel brighten a contemporary kitchen addition, while wood flooring and flat-panel Shaker cabinet doors add a traditional touch. Wall cabinets abut the ceiling to offer more storage space; frosted glass keeps contents looking tidy.

RIGHT A stunning two-story space makes this country kitchen transcend its cozy style with wood cabinets designed to look like a collection of individual furniture pieces.

• traditional styles

Traditional kitchens come in many styles, but they all aim to reproduce the details and ambience of domestic architecture before the mid-20th century, or at least our romantic view of houses from bygone eras. As a rule, a traditional kitchen will have more ornate molding than will a modern design, and cabinetry will have frame-and-panel doors. Specific styles call for particular details, such as inset quartersawn oak doors on Craftsman-style cabinets. A traditional country kitchen will have an unfitted look, with furniture-style legs, a variety of finishes, and varying height countertops rather than banks of same-size cabinets.

Traditionally styled custom cabinetry features frame-and-panel doors and furniture feet, with a bit of flourish on the built-in china cabinet at the left. Rustic beams and a warm wood floor nail down the traditional style.

BELOW For a truly traditional look, forgo the toe space at the base cabinets, as seen in this beautiful Maine kitchen. The countertop projects past the cabinet to make it comfortable to stand.

ABOVE Open shelves can be a traditional detail and a lighter, brighter alternative to a string of wall cabinets (they're easier to access, too). These wood shelves with hidden supports look streamlined, but the overall effect of the kitchen is country.

ABOVE Prairie-style frame-and-panel doors and matching panels on the dishwasher and refrigerator get traditional visual support from the rest of the kitchen by way of decorative cutouts, curved wood brackets, and a well-matched pendant light fixture.

RIGHT This charming Connecticut kitchen virtually raises its low, 19th-century ceiling by focusing color and deep tone on the floor, keeping the rest of the kitchen white, and filling walls with open shelves. Traditional beadboard paneling, marble countertops, frame-and-panel doors, and curvy brackets set the style.

DIGGING AN ELEGANT KITCHEN
OUT OF THE BASEMENT

Perfectly suited for a 19th-century Brooklyn townhouse, this completely redone kitchen is traditional in style and detailing, with a farmhouse sink, nickel bin pulls, wall cabinets with glass doors, classic diamond-tile flooring, and granite countertops. The bench at the right is an up-to-date live-in-the-kitchen bonus.

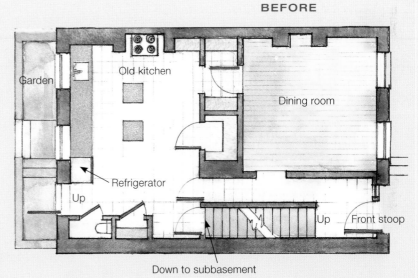

BEFORE

Garden

Old kitchen

Dining room

Refrigerator

Up

Down to subbasement

Up   Front stoop

The interior of the basement as shown in this plan was all removed down to the masonry walls.

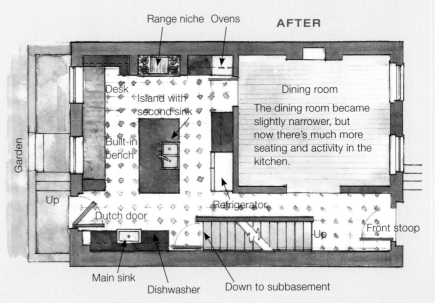

Range niche   Ovens

AFTER

Desk

Island with second sink

Built-in bench

Garden

Up

Dutch door

Dining room

The dining room became slightly narrower, but now there's much more seating and activity in the kitchen.

Refrigerator

Down to subbasement

Up   Front stoop

Main sink   Dishwasher

As new interior walls were built, the kitchen was replumbed, rewired, and fit up with new a HVAC system; radiant heat was added to the floor before tiles were installed.

With the stairs removed, light makes its way inside via the Dutch door.

• modern kitchens

Modern kitchen design calls to mind sleek detailing, smooth surfaces, recessed lighting, and full-flush doors in frameless cabinets, sometimes with tall, Euro-style toespaces, and often with simple drawers and doors. Gleaming, synthetic materials, such as stainless steel, glass tile, and composites may be the finishes of choice in a modern kitchen, but traditional materials and matte finishes can easily take on a modern cast if designed with clean, linear details. In fact, it's not the material but the detailing that makes a modern- or contemporary-style kitchen.

BELOW Contemporary rosewood cabinets barely skim the ceiling in this renovated urban kitchen. Crisp detailing includes square-edged white quartz countertops, white glass backsplashes, and a sleek faucet.

ABOVE This contemporary kitchen in a San Antonio carriage house is minimalist but not reserved. Its Texas-sunshine orange wall cabinets are cooled by gray base cabinets, backsplash, and countertop.

FACING PAGE Discretion defines this modern-style kitchen, from the full-overlay flat-slab cabinet doors and drawers with subtle thumb pulls to the streamlined continuous cove with hidden lighting.

• eclectic and transitional kitchens

Transitional-style kitchens mix traditional and modern elements in a balanced and subtle way, often with a palette of neutral colors. A rustic mosaic tile backsplash could complement gray flat-slab cabinets with frosted-glass door panels, for example. An eclectic kitchen tends to tilt toward a more-surprising, less-restrained contrast, perhaps with sleek appliances balanced by bright colors or ornate cabinetry. In both kinds of kitchens, it's the mix of styles that sets the style.

Traditional and contemporary elements pair up to make a kitchen both elegant and eclectic. The red antler chandelier and bold wallpaper are tempered by solid tones of dark hevea wood floor, faux baby ostrich leather–covered walls, and matte charcoal kitchen cabinets. The marble Saarinen-designed tulip table doubles as a comfortable workspace for the owner-architect, who uses a wheelchair.

ABOVE What gives this butler's pantry its style is a contemporary twist on frame-and-panel doors, with unusually sleek, wide frames. The prominent vertical joint and contemporary pulls are balanced by traditional butt hinges and marble countertop.

ABOVE In a coastal Maine kitchen, the bygone era of sailing ships is recalled in a hand-painted mural that fills all cabinet panels. The birch cabinet frames are painted with exaggerated faux wood grain. Modern solid-surface countertops and crisp detailing balance the nod to the past.

layout: the kitchen triangle still adds up

● ● ● THE CLASSIC KITCHEN TRIANGLE COUNTS the range, the sink, and a refrigerator as its points, each with their adjacent workspaces. Ideally, the legs of that triangle—the total distance between the three points—will add up to between 12 ft. and 26 ft. overall. But don't sweat a few inches, or even feet. Just keep in mind that the goal of the kitchen triangle is to remind you to keep the primary elements of the kitchen reasonably close together to make it efficient, safe, and easy to prepare foods, serve dinner, and clean up afterward. It's important to locate countertop space where you need it: a landing space near the fridge, prep space near the cooktop, and room for dirty pots and pans next to the sink, or even in the sink if you have a second sink for prepping. See Chapter 6 for countertop guidelines.

The landing space for items from the refrigerator is actually the island countertop (especially when cooking is going on), and from there it's a short hop to the sink, then to the cooktop. There's enough space at the island for a second cook.

f you're at odds with your current kitchen but there's no time for a complete makeover, contemplate some quick function upgrades to improve your layout. Add cabinet inserts such as small lazy Susans for spices, tilt-out bins, and wire racks that sort utensils and condiments. Remove fixed shelves and replace them with pull-out shelves. Add a portable butcher-block-topped island to a kitchen that has either too little countertop space or counters too far apart. In a claustrophobic kitchen, remove a bank of upper cabinets and replace them with a few open shelves or none at all. Change the swing of an annoying door so that it opens away from traffic.

ABOVE This big kitchen has two wall ovens, a cooktop, two dishwashers, and a coffee station in addition to a big refrigerator-freezer. Food prep is centered on this corner, keeping the cooking area fairly compact.

RIGHT A dining table on wheels liberates this kitchen so multiple cooks can help with dinner preparation. The overlapping work stations, second sink, second oven, and the option of enlisting all sides of the island and even the table for kitchen duty boost efficiency.

green ideas...
FOR STYLE
AND LAYOUT

t hinking green is no longer a trend—it's mainstream. The term *green* applies to products, processes, and design practices that save energy and resources, and promote health. Look for green suggestions throughout the book and consider these green basics:

- For the most substantial green impact, invest in cubic footage rather than square footage and build a smaller but smarter kitchen.

- Select cabinet, countertop, and flooring materials that use less energy to produce and use fewer chemicals to install and maintain; consider salvaged materials.

- Focus on appliances: Locate the range or cooktop on an outside wall to make it simpler and less expensive to duct the fan, and use a ducted fan, not a circulating fan, for health and safety. In very cold climates, locate plumbing on interior walls. Separate your refrigerator and range so that one appliance doesn't diminish the effectiveness of the other, and keep the fridge out of direct sun, if possible. New energy-efficient appliances can reduce your energy bill.

- If you are building a house from scratch, rely on natural light—and fresh air—as much as possible by designing in lots of operable windows, perhaps even instead of a bank of wall cabinets, and use energy-efficient light fixtures where artificial light is necessary.

ABOVE A prep sink creates a short-legged triangle between refrigerator, island, and cooktop, while the big sink overlooking the fields operates as a fourth workstation after dinner, or as a second workspace for a multicook kitchen.

ABOVE This cozy cottage lays claim to a compact kitchen triangle; it takes just one or two steps to move from refrigerator (facing the range but out of view here) to sink to range and back. A welcoming peninsula keeps a sitter or two out of the kitchen but at hand for prep tasks or company.

ABOVE This kitchen triangle has morphed into a straight line between range, sink, and fridge, but the big pantry at the left and a generous, unencumbered island make the kitchen highly functional, even for two cooks.

BELOW This compressed triangle between fridge, sink, and cooktop is short and sweet, and meant for a solo cook. Keeping the kitchen focused on just sides allows the third wall to be almost all window.

more about...
BENDING THE TRIANGLE

not all kitchen layouts conform to a single triangle. The range may be split into wall ovens and a cooktop, the primary sink may be supplemented by a prep or bar sink, and a microwave oven and perhaps a warming oven may be added. When second appliances are put into the picture, keep them relatively close, ideally between 4 ft. and 9 ft. away. Doubling up on appliances is especially helpful for a two-or-more-cook kitchen. Even a refrigerator can be split into a separate fridge and freezer or supplemented by refrigerator drawers positioned out of the cook's path.

more about...
EASIER RECYCLING

determine how many bins you need, then consider where to store them. You can dump recyclables from a small kitchen bin into a bigger bin that's stored near the kitchen or outside. Although it's common to locate garbage and/or recycling under the sink, that can become a source of conflict. Instead, locate garbage or recycling bins on one side of the wash-up sink and the dishwasher on the other. Or locate garbage across the aisle but not in a major path. Locate additional garbage or compost bins close to food prep. Make any garbage or recycling cabinet easy to open, perhaps with your foot or with a touch-latch.

sizing kitchen layouts

● ● ● A SOLO COOK WILL WORK HAPPILY IN a galley with a 38-in.-wide aisle, but if a second cook pitches in, it'll be hard to keep from bumping hips in such a narrow space. For an active kitchen, make aisles 42 in. wide—even better 48 in. wide—especially if complicated meals are your forte. This extra width allows drawers, dishwasher, and refrigerator to be opened with ease, and offers passing room for two cooks. Add even more space if one side of the aisle backs up to a seating area. Spectators and other noncooks often want to get to the fridge and sometimes to the microwave, so place those two appliances at the edges of the kitchen's heavy-duty workspace, not in the center.

Locate items where you will use them: Put baking supplies and mixer together under or near the countertop where you knead bread. Store cereals, bowls, coffee-making supplies, and other breakfast items near where you eat in the kitchen, whether breakfast nook or island. Store cooking utensils (spatulas, wooden spoons, tongs, and the like) within close reach of the cooktop, either on hooks and visible or at hand in a drawer; locate pot holders near the oven. Plan for dish storage near the dishwasher or, if you prefer, near the space where you will be plating the food for serving. If it works for your space and needs, locate the serving spot between the cooking and the dishwasher/sink areas. There may be exceptions to these rules, so analyze your needs. If you have a cold wall and space for a pantry, that could be the best place to store flour rather than in the heat of the kitchen.

A bachelor cook wastes no energy in his tiny urban kitchen, with sink, two-burner smooth cooktop, dishwasher, refrigerator and freezer drawers, and wall-mounted high-speed oven all close at hand. Top cabinets store less-used items. The countertop is Calacatta Gold marble.

A kitchen designed for a wheelchair user can look just as fashionable and livable as any kitchen. In fact, it's more livable, as a lowered countertop with room to sit at the sink can be a boon for anyone. And slightly wider aisles and easy-to-operate hardware make working in the kitchen a joy. A variety of countertop heights makes the kitchen more flexible too.

UNIVERSAL DESIGN IS FOR EVERYONE

universal design—also called barrier-free design, aging-in-place design, or simply accessible design—is all about making built spaces easier on everyone, no matter the age, health, or ability. There's no stigma attached to universal design guidelines. In fact, they are just plain common sense, and you've seen them in action. You'll find specific universal design concepts throughout this book, but start with these basic suggestions as you think about your own kitchen:

- Make aisles at least 42 in. (48 in. is even better) for a two-cook work area, and provide a 5-ft.-dia. clear space somewhere to allow a wheelchair to turn around.
- Replace a fixed island with a moveable island; even a simple table with four legs and no side braces, or supplement a fixed island with a rolling cart. A moveable island can be pushed aside to make room for a walker or

wheelchair, and it not only offers a flexible workspace but can double as a buffet table.

- Choose full-extension hardware for drawers and pull-out shelves to make storage more accessible, and select easy-to-grip pulls and knobs instead of streamlined pull cylinders and tabs. For doors, lever handles are easier to operate than knob handles.
- It's easiest to retrieve and put away items that are stored between 15 in. and 48 in. above the floor, but your span may vary, depending on height and comfortable range of motion.
- Provide more than one countertop height to make a variety of kitchen tasks easier and to make it easier for people of different heights to work comfortably. For example, it's more comfortable to knead and roll out dough on lower surfaces, while some fine-motor tasks are easier on higher surfaces.

- For washing up, a shallow sink is easier to reach into, and a single-lever faucet is much simpler and quicker to operate than a two-handle faucet.
- Appliance configurations and elevations make a difference. A side-by-side refrigerator is easier to access than any other configuration except for refrigerator and freezer drawers, but drawers are considerably more expensive per cubic foot. A wall oven is easier to operate than a range oven because it is elevated above the floor; a microwave oven is easier and safer to access when it is located lower than usual.
- Keep flooring smooth, and avoid throw rugs.
- Provide lighting for every work surface, preferably from more than one source to avoid harsh shadows, and make lighting adjustable. A bright kitchen is not only safer but more cheerful.

a good fit with the house

●●● THANKS TO EFFECTIVE COOKTOP ventilation and a change in family dynamics, the kitchen long ago came out of the shadows and into top billing in today's homes, but you may still want to reinforce its open relationship to living spaces and to the outdoors. Connecting the kitchen to living areas can be as simple as carving out a pass-through or widening a doorway, or it can entail the major overhaul of combining both spaces into one great room. A parent who works from home may appreciate an office next to the kitchen, and might be happy to share it with kids doing homework. Opening a kitchen to the living space means paying attention to appearances. The kitchen can be designed either to blend, with similar materials, or to contrast, with a change of ceiling heights, materials, and colors. It's harder to blend a kitchen in with living space because it's not an easy beast to camouflage, and the kitchen warrants tougher finishes for durability and ease of cleaning. But you can hide appliances behind panels that match the cabinetry. An intermediate ceiling-hung cabinet can provide a subtle screen and provide space for display.

An urban kitchen for a young family demands a connection between kitchen and living spaces. Seating makes it possible to see the television. The cooktop is farther from the fray for safety. The 24-ft.-long island sets up an excellent throughway for scootering.

LEFT This new cottage is home to a retired couple who downsized square footage but not convenience. The kitchen shares space with the living room, with pot rack and range hood as visual separation. The hood is essential for the couple's high-intensity cooking style.

BELOW A kitchen redo added cubbies between the back door and the kitchen to make it easier for the family to keep organized without encroaching on precious kitchen work space.

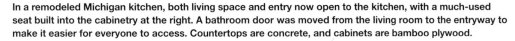

In a remodeled Michigan kitchen, both living space and entry now open to the kitchen, with a much-used seat built into the cabinetry at the right. A bathroom door was moved from the living room to the entryway to make it easier for everyone to access. Countertops are concrete, and cabinets are bamboo plywood.

ABOVE It's a straight shot from the mudroom (behind the sliding frosted door in the background) to the deck, just this side of the dining space. The path through the kitchen avoids the heavy-duty cooking workspace.

RIGHT This elegant kitchen is neatly tucked into the framework of the house's prominent post-and-beam structure, and within the kitchen, the butler's pantry is nearly transparent, keeping light and view unobstructed, at least above base cabinet level. Robin's egg blue makes an inviting accent color for the peninsula, which has a high wood counter to shield the sink.

A family kitchen ideally has space for work by all ages. This dedicated two-seater desk means no one has to clean up to make room for food prep or dinner.

The original kitchen in this early 1970s home actually faced away from the windows and was divided into several cramped workspaces. A redo knocked down walls to open up to both the living space and the outdoors.

• link up with the outdoors

No one will ever want to leave a kitchen with a great view. The view could be of an active living space or it could be a view of the outdoors, whether it's kids playing in the backyard, clouds above distant mountains, or the sparkle of a lake or ocean. Can you see that view when preparing a meal? How about when washing up? You may have to choose one task over another to command the sight line. And have you considered where to locate a warm-weather outdoor eating space so that it's convenient to the kitchen? A screened porch will be in constant use if it's easy to access from the kitchen. If the porch abuts the kitchen, make the porch ceiling high and the shared windows tall to allow more light into the kitchen. You can add skylights to a screened porch for even more light. The approach to the porch should not be straight through the hardworking part of the kitchen. Two doors would be great, one for the cooks heading back and forth to the grill (which is likely not inside the porch) and a second door that allows family and friends to move around independently.

Although it's still a few feet below the garden, this completely redone kitchen is bright and cheery. A Dutch door adds charm and adjustable access to the outdoors.

A new addition to a suburban Minneapolis home added both kitchen and dining space and a sunny screened porch. Its proximity to the kitchen makes the porch a popular place.

Two back doors open up a kitchen to the glories of a Portland, Oregon, summer day. Dining snugs up close to the window wall to enjoy the view. A more practical door at the right makes for easy access in and out.

FACING PAGE An energy-efficient kitchen is a just-right size, with an easy walk between fridge, sink, and cooktop-cum-undercabinet oven. A downdraft hood and pop-up electrical receptacles keep the vista clear. The countertop is EcoTop®, a blend of recycled and bamboo fibers and lighting is via LED and CFL bulbs. The pantry is finished with family-friendly chalkboard paint.

LEFT If possible, give built-in seating a view of the outdoors, as in this kitchen redo. A generous arched opening frames the view and allows light to bounce off white painted surfaces.

the kitchen island

• • •

THE KITCHEN ISLAND HAS BEEN AROUND FOR A LONG TIME, IN THE form of the sturdy kitchen table, but the mid-20th-century trend toward smaller kitchens squeezed it out. Then kitchens got larger, and the built-in island was born with a nod toward the commercial kitchen's central prep-space, and it's been a prime player in home kitchens since. Especially in a larger kitchen, the island makes a lot of sense. A large kitchen takes more steps from one point to another, and an island can offer an intermediate counter space for more efficiency. If several cooks are working at once, an island's extra surface is especially welcome. The island allows the cook to turn around and interact with others, but it also acts as a buffer and shields traffic.

As with the kitchen, there is no perfect island. It's up to you and your budget and space to decide its size, contents, and materials. A simple kitchen table might be just the ticket because you can sit down to work at it or stand up and it's the perfect height for kneading bread. But more often than not, the kitchen island contains loads of storage, often an appliance or two, and offers a place to sit.

An island can make a kitchen more efficient, and flexible. The original kitchen island was a simple table, not quite as elegant or as full of storage possibilities as this one. But it was moveable, allowing the kitchen to change with the season or the meal.

The island is the ideal spot for adding lighting that's both functional and decorative, such as a line of pendants, a chandelier, or a bar with spotlights. Island lighting helps brighten a kitchen's midpoint without having to speckle the ceiling with recessed can lighting. You may want to downplay the island by matching its finishes to the rest of the kitchen, but why not make the island a design counterpoint, with contrasting countertop and cabinet color and materials?

islands that stay put

●●● ALTHOUGH A BUILT-IN ISLAND CAN BE AS simple as a countertop plopped onto a cluster of cabinets facing one way, it can also practically be a kitchen in itself, with everything—including the kitchen sink. Of course, a sink and any appliances in an island require plumbing, wiring, and possibly ductwork. Built-in islands require electrical receptacles at code-required locations, so take time early on to figure exact locations and trim materials rather than having receptacles plugged in as afterthoughts. A two-height island countertop offers an ideal surface at a handy location, perfect for using a mixer or other small kitchen appliance. Two-tiered island countertops also suit different kitchen tasks, and cook heights; they can shield the less lovely parts of kitchen work from diners, and can make it safer for diners to sit near a cooktop. But a one-level countertop with no interrupting sink or appliance makes the perfect surface for holiday baking or laying out a buffet. You can have the built-in look and convenience of storage but avoid the need for electrical receptacles by building a big island with true legs, not to-the-floor cabinet bases.

While not strictly an island, the aisle just that side of the wall makes it easy to move around, like an island, and its marble waterfall countertop is detailed island-style. A solid bank of sleek cabinets is broken by double-hung windows with marble shelves floating across them.

BELOW It may be small, but this fixed island has room for a microwave drawer, and its marble countertop can act as either a landing space or a workspace.

BELOW A two-level island with quartz countertops provides a view during washing, while the raised countertop acts as both a breakfast bar and a shield for sink activities. The family's two boys shift back and forth between the bar stools and the built-in bench, which is fit up with drawers packed with toys.

more about...
SIZING ISLANDS

eep the aisle between an island and the perimeter cabinets at a width that suits your kitchen space and your cooking habits. A single-cook aisle can be 42 in. wide, whereas two cooks will work more harmoniously with a 46-in. to 60-in aisle. That wider space is especially important when appliance doors are open. Allow at least 60 in. between an island and an adjacent dining table. An island with a healthy girth will force cooks to do more walking, so it may make sense to fill an especially large central space with two separate islands. Avoid placing an island between two points of the kitchen triangle so you don't have to walk around it to get from refrigerator to sink, for example. While the standard countertop is 36 in. high, there's no reason why your island can't be as low or as high as you'd like, whether for dining at bar or table height or for various cooking tasks. See Chapter 6 for suggested countertop heights and widths.

RIGHT A major overhaul, this lovely, light-filled kitchen has a freestanding but massive island at its center. The cantilevered marble countertop is supported by curved brackets in sync with abundant traditionally styled cabinetry. Glass cabinetry at right is also accessible from the dining room. Once concealed by linoleum, the original Douglas fir floor was stained dark in contrast.

ABOVE A modest kitchen island makes space for dining but converts to a workspace when the bar stools tuck below the countertop. The low-maintenance countertop is engineered stone.

BELOW This giant island is kitchen on one side, living room on the other, with thick-edged shelves for books and objects and two-person bar seating. The ebony-stained floor and island base create a stunning and solid foundation in contrast to all the white.

FOR AN OLD ISLAND

as with any cabinets, it's possible to upgrade island storage with new hardware, fresh paint, or refaced doors and drawers. And, of course, you can upgrade any island appliances, as long as they fit. But what about the countertop? That's possible to change out, too, and here's where you can make a functional upgrade to an island by adding square footage to the top without changing the island's footprint, enough for bar seating, for example. But this strategy works only if the cabinets are deemed to be strong enough for a bigger, probably heavier, countertop and only if the new, deeper countertop can be properly supported; ask for an expert opinion. And do make sure your bigger island doesn't make an aisle too narrow. A change in another direction is to beef up or upgrade island lighting with a decorative chandelier, better task lighting, more efficient lighting, or all three.

the moveable island

● ● ● A MOVEABLE ISLAND MAKES FOR A MORE flexible kitchen layout, a big plus if you are aiming to improve accessibility because the island can be shifted to allow space for a wheelchair to pass. And a moveable island that's table height offers sit-down workspace for food preparation. A floating island can't contain a sink or appliance, but that means you'll be saving money. Such islands can still contain loads of storage if you don't mind losing the sitting space. Be sure any suspended light fixtures over a moveable island are higher than your head in case you do relocate the island.

FACING PAGE A small house in New England built for super-high energy efficiency calls on human power to reposition this island on wheels, whether to serve as a supplemental workspace or as a buffet table.

RIGHT This chunky face-grain butcher-block island table does double-duty as a casual dining table and a workspace. Two drawers on each side can hold small kitchen tools or napkins.

LEFT These two islands can work in tandem to provide workspace, dining space, or both. It's easy to pull up stools to the rolling butcher-block table, just as easy to stand and work, and a breeze to move to another location.

•island storage

Island storage is the exact opposite of corner cabinet storage—it's twice as easy to reach. That all-sides-available feature of an island allows for access to storage from different places and for different needs. Consider a combination of closed and open storage, fixed and pull-out shelves, and drawers of all sizes. Be aware that an island is like a three-dimensional puzzle in which all the parts have to fit, so it's not always possible to include storage on all sides. Finish nonstorage sides with decorative panels, tile, or beadboard if that suits, or use nonstorage sides for dining space. Keep cooking gear on the prep side and dishes, place mats, and the like on the dining/living side to improve efficiency. While a curved island can make for smoother traffic patterns, curved cabinetry is expensive. The solution is easy: curve just the countertop, not the cabinets. The resulting surface overhang can be a handy sitting spot if it's deep enough.

FACING PAGE, TOP This island's standard cabinet storage flanking the sink is supplemented at each end by open storage for decorative or oversize items.

All it takes for workable shelving is a 6-in. to 8-in. depth, as seen in this New England island. The countertop curves out to make a more generous dining space.

This island looks built in, but it's not because it has true legs and nothing is holding it in place but gravity. Substantial shelves and lots of drawers make for a highly functional piece of furniture, along with a marble countertop open to food preparation, serving, and dining.

An island makes an ideal spot for cookbook shelves, especially when there's room nearby for doing some barstool recipe reading.

•island sinks

If you need additional workspace, a second sink can turn an island into a handy food-prep area, especially if it's located not far from the fridge and across from the cooktop. But you might want to compromise a bit on location and shift the sink toward one end rather than plunking it right in the middle of the island where it could chop up the surface too much. Chalk out your dimensions on an island-size piece of cardboard—an appliance box is ideal—and spend some time mulling over the layout. Because an island is usually the focus of a kitchen, a big wash-up sink with a dishwasher will put dirty dishes on center stage. Consider popping up the countertop on the side facing the living/dining space. The raised counter makes a great height for bar seating.

Two islands provide all of the countertop space, while a solid back wall of aluminum-paneled cabinets conceals all the storage and contains most of the appliances. The farther island includes a cooktop and the closer island is home to two sink basins, a hot/cold faucet, and a purified water faucet. An elm-veneered countertop offers bar seating with a window view.

ABOVE Primary for food prep and breakfast washup, this two-bowl undermount sink is an island backup to the prime sink, a large farmhouse-style model that handles big pans.

RIGHT Maple butcher block with a curved front and seating for six makes for a warm and welcoming island countertop. The countertop is 1½ in. thick at each end but thinner at the undermounted sink to keep the basin from being too low. Hollow island legs act as chases for wiring. The island sink is a straight-edged two-bowl model with a serious, restaurant-style faucet.

ABOVE A small cottage has a streamlined but elegant kitchen, with a narrow fridge (at center right in the background) and a single-bowl undermount sink in the marble-topped dining and food-prep island.

• island appliances

A center island might be just the spot for appliances, whether on the working side of the island or the noncook side. If the range or cooktop and ovens are positioned on a wall, consider locating a microwave oven or warming oven in the island cabinetry so that it's closer to noncooks and easier to reach. A below-counter refrigerator and refrigerator drawers are perfect candidates for island duty so hungry family members can retrieve cold beverages and snacks without interfering with cooking tasks. Be aware that the appliance door will open onto the aisle, so leave enough room so it can be open and still allow people to walk by.

It's easier to ventilate and safer to cook on a cooktop located against a wall, but you may prefer the cooktop or range to be installed in an island. If so, make it a safe location. Include a heatproof landing space on all three sides of the cooktop, at least 15 in. on the sides and either a broad expanse on the far side or a low wall or raised countertop. A higher countertop offers not only protection from spatters and steam but a perfect spot to plate a meal. A pop-up exhaust system can be sufficient for cooks who aren't obsessed with high-heat cooking, but a range hood is much more efficient, can be a great design feature, and provides the task lighting that a cooktop requires. Don't put off choosing appliances because cabinetry and any electrical and plumbing layouts depend on the specifications of the appliances you select.

The island cooktop is well served by a range hood. Island cabinets open toward the cook for easy access, while the cabinets that open toward bar seating are for less-used items. The cabinets are Shaker style, and the rust-colored backsplash is end-grain mesquite laid like brickwork.

Once a dark, cramped kitchen, this bright space features a massive island that houses an oven and a cooktop with a powerful range hood, an important feature because island cooking is harder to vent.

ABOVE A chunky butcher block makes a casual dining bar on a two-level island, and it helps block cooking splatters.

LEFT An island helps turn around kitchen work so the cook or scullery crew can visit with family or friends or enjoy a beautiful view. This island does both, allowing the cook to face the wide double-doors that open to the deck and a view of the North Carolina mountains. The floors are ash, the trim is pine, and the cabinets are from IKEA.

dining and work spaces

• • •

A HEART-OF-THE-HOUSE KITCHEN ALWAYS ATTRACTS A CROWD. AN occasional cook may prefer solitude, but other family members and friends will drift into the kitchen anyway, so why not make room for them? Dedicated space for eating in or near the kitchen makes sense for busy people, for easy cleanup, and for just plain coziness. Cooking style, family size, and how the kitchen connects to the rest of the house and the outdoors will determine how and where dining gets incorporated into the kitchen. In-kitchen dining can be as casual as pulling a few stools up to a 36-in.-high island countertop or carving out space for a breakfast nook or a standard dining table. While considering space for eating, think about other noncooking tasks done in the kitchen. Almost every family needs space for working at a computer or paying household bills. A place for kids to do supervised homework is a bonus. Such workspaces should be sheltered from high-intensity cooking but allow for quick access to what's cooking in the likely case you're multitasking. Sometimes there's not even a need for a table, just space for a comfy chair, a couch to stretch out on, or a built-in bench to sit on while reading, talking, doing homework, or in the case of a window seat, enjoying the view. A big enough bench can double as sleeping space when cousins come to visit, and it makes a fine spot for eating a midnight snack.

This sun-filled breakfast nook is light-years away from the dark corner it used to be as part of a cramped kitchen. The room's few scrawny windows were popped out and replaced with large windows that capture hillside views. A built-in bamboo seat offers ample storage space under the seat lid.

eating in the kitchen

● ● ● A SPACIOUS DINING ROOM IS GREAT FOR dinner parties and holidays, but today's packed schedules often don't include time to set a dining room table for everyday meals, so in-kitchen dining has become the norm for many. The simplest approach to eating in the kitchen is to make room for a table and chairs. Built-in dining can add a sense of security and coziness, and a breakfast nook is often a favorite place to eat. Bar seating is easier to get to, though, and bar stools can be tucked away or removed when the bar countertop transforms to food-preparation or buffet space. Although built-in counters and seats are great for staking out a permanent claim, moveable furniture does make it easier to take over the entire kitchen for food preparation during feast times and can allow more chairs to be pulled up for a bigger crowd. A combination of built-in and moveable dining may be just the ticket. For any dining space, pay the same attention to lighting kitchen dining spaces as you would a formal dining room, with a focus on task and ambient lighting, often by pendant fixtures or directed lighting.

Whatever the eat-in dining configuration you choose, think about how close you want it to food prep. An undercabinet refrigerator just for diners can keep people from getting underfoot, or position the refrigerator/freezer in the zone between cooking and seating. A perimeter microwave can help guide traffic away from the main cooking area too.

This big kitchen has plenty of room for the extended family at Thanksgiving, if you count the window seat across the hall. Generous natural light bounces off the ceiling via clerestory windows, while food prep and dining pendants provide stylish light to suit the purpose.

ABOVE This mahogany island offers bar seating for two or three on the living room side. In the window niche is a large dining table that seats up to 16 on both an L-shaped banquette and chairs.

BELOW A view over the city demands a dining bar like this one. Flanking mahogany cabinets provide storage for linens and dishware, and shallow drawers under the countertop hold flatware.

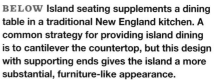

BELOW Island seating supplements a dining table in a traditional New England kitchen. A common strategy for providing island dining is to cantilever the countertop, but this design with supporting ends gives the island a more substantial, furniture-like appearance.

more about...
THE DINING ROOM: IS IT A DINOSAUR?

You may never miss having a formal dining room if there's room in the kitchen for a standard dining table and enough chairs for family and guests. In a kitchen with a great view, locate table and chairs close to the windows rather than taking up that space with cabinetry. A cook can always look up from work to see over a dining table to the outdoors. A dining alcove can be finished in softer, less durable materials than the rest of the kitchen—just like a formal dining room.

make elbow room for comfortable dining

t he National Kitchen & Bath Association recommends that for seating where no through traffic passes behind the diner, allow 32 in. between the table or countertop edge and the nearest vertical wall or vertical obstruction. If traffic does pass behind the seated diner, increase that dimension to 44 in. for a comfortable walkthrough, or just 36 in. if you don't mind squeezing. For countertop height, depth, and width, see the chart below.

	COUNTER HEIGHT	KNEE-SPACE DEPTH	WIDTH PER SEAT	SEAT HEIGHT
Table dining	28 in. to 30 in.	18 in.	24 in.	18 in. to 19 in.
Standard countertop height	36 in.	15 in.	24 in.	24 in. to 26 in.
Bar height	42 in.	12 in.	24 in.	30 in.
Universal design access for wheelchair	27 in. to 34 in.	17 in. at feet; 11 in. at knees	36 in.	N/A

ABOVE The end of this small island is open to allow for a couple of bar stools with low backs, making it easy to work as well as eat. The countertop is engineered quartz.

FACING PAGE Benches and table provide space for dining in this California kitchen; the raised bar offers additional space during big family gatherings or parties, and it shields the cooktop too.

RIGHT A tiny table for two pops up for dinner by the window, or it can be a workspace by day or night. When the table isn't in use, it swings down and lies flush with the cabinets.

built-in dining

● ● ● BUILT-IN SEATING IS IDEAL FOR corralling the littlest kids and for making them feel snug; it makes adults feel cozy, too. Built-in seating can be designed like a booth with two benches facing each other or with benches in an L- or U-shape. U-shaped banquettes are wonderfully cozy, and allow you to squeeze in one more person, but they are also hard to climb into, and somehow the first person in always needs to get out first. Aesthetically, built-in seats can help shape a room. Because it is low, broad, and deep, a breakfast booth can be a strong and appealing visual ballast without blocking the view between rooms or to the outdoors.

A combination of built-in and chair seating allows more flexibility in table size and position, and allows a high-chair or a wheelchair to fit at the table. For booth and U-shaped seating, and sometimes L-shaped, choose a pedestal table that won't interfere with getting in and out. A freestanding table can be moved out for easier cleaning. For the times when the breakfast nook becomes the homework or workstation, provide nearby outlets for laptops and a way to deal with cords.

RIGHT When a dark back entrance was opened up and incorporated into the kitchen, one of the bonus built-ins was this cozy window seat. Bamboo-and-glass cabinets hold shoes, boots, and kitchen goods.

FAR RIGHT Just a few steps up from a big family kitchen is a family room/study room with built-in seating and a desk. Two ways in and out keep traffic collisions to a minimum.

This cozy breakfast booth has a prime spot in a bump-out so it takes advantage of windows on three sides (the left window opens onto the mudroom). Beadboard wainscoting and ceiling and an arched opening make the booth seem part of a formal Victorian porch.

more about...
MAKING BUILT-IN SEATING COMFORTABLE

a built-in bench for seating should feel like a comfortable chair (see "Sizing Built-in Dining" on p. 65). Feet should touch the floor, you should be able to lean back, but not too far, and the seat edge shouldn't cut into the back of your knees. A comfortable seat bottom overhangs the bench front, if there is one, a few inches so that your legs have room to move. For the most comfort, pitch the seat back 5° or slightly more, or pitch the seat itself along with the seat back. Allow a few inches beyond the seat back for your head. Add a few more inches to make room for shelves, one side or two, for a display space for favorite objects or a library for cookbooks. That's only if your breakfast nook is not by a window. If you have the option for windows, take it. If the windows are low and there's a possibility someone will bang into them, make sure the glass is tempered. To make it more comfortable for people to slip in and out of a corner bench, gently round the corners of the table.

ABOVE Designed to be big enough to sleep two grown-ups for short stays, this L-shaped built-in seating doubles as a dining area for a small beach house. Wide-board paneling makes for a seaside-worthy wall finish.

RIGHT A big house in Portland, OR, gathers living, dining, and kitchen in one big space but the timber-frame structure gives each area its own character. This big table offers half standard dining and half built-in, so there's always room for one more.

BUILT-IN
STORAGE SPACE

b uilt-in seating offers an opportunity for storage, but be practical. A hinged top over a bin is a common feature, but what will you store there? This could be a great place for items that are big or seasonal, such as extra throws or pillows, but only if it's easy to open the seat lid and remove big items. Just don't allow a storage bin to be a catch all for things of any size. And built-in seat bins in houses with small children should be lockable so kids aren't tempted to hide for fun. An expensive, but much more accessible storage option is to fit up a built-in seat with drawers that can be opened from the ends facing out. An alternative is to simply design built-in seating as a bench, which can then be kept clear underneath or filled with like-size baskets or good-looking boxes, with handles for easy access.

Built-in seating adds character and comfort to a kitchen, and it also adds storage space. It's more expensive to build in drawers than to make the seat a lid for trunk-like storage, but drawers are much easier to access.

ABOVE The most used spot in this handsome kitchen redo is a long built-in bench against an outside wall. The bench is used for cookbook reading, work, eating, talking, and napping.

LEFT A family of five often eats all meals in this breakfast nook, designed to fit the house's original Craftsman character, sadly ignored by a 1970s redo. Under-seat drawers offer easy-to-access storage. An island with a soapstone countertop contains the prep sink. The narrow fridge—one of two instead of one oversize model—is close to dining to lighten traffic.

ABOVE The flat-screen television is here to stay, so it could make sense to center a built-in dining area around it. When the TV is off, the outdoors provides a lovely view. The table can be moved for flexibility.

RIGHT A magnetic chalkboard backing this dining niche says it's time for breakfast, but any meal would taste great here. A few chunky steps up from the kitchen level is a deck for entertaining, enjoying the outdoors, or taking in the sights of the Boston neighborhood.

SIZING BUILT-IN DINING

A breakfast nook with benches requires a pedestal or trestle table, or in a two-sided booth like this, the table can be supported by the wall on one end and a central leg near the other end.

THE TRADITIONAL BREAKFAST BOOTH

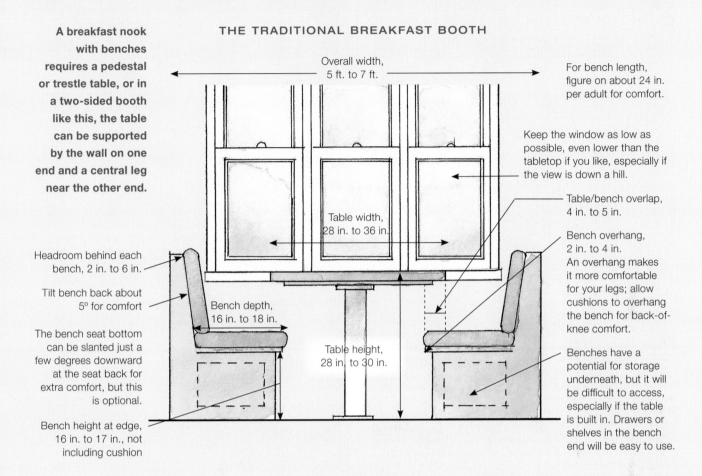

Overall width, 5 ft. to 7 ft.

For bench length, figure on about 24 in. per adult for comfort.

Keep the window as low as possible, even lower than the tabletop if you like, especially if the view is down a hill.

Table width, 28 in. to 36 in.

Table/bench overlap, 4 in. to 5 in.

Bench overhang, 2 in. to 4 in. An overhang makes it more comfortable for your legs; allow cushions to overhang the bench for back-of-knee comfort.

Headroom behind each bench, 2 in. to 6 in.

Tilt bench back about 5° for comfort

Bench depth, 16 in. to 18 in.

Table height, 28 in. to 30 in.

The bench seat bottom can be slanted just a few degrees downward at the seat back for extra comfort, but this is optional.

Benches have a potential for storage underneath, but it will be difficult to access, especially if the table is built in. Drawers or shelves in the bench end will be easy to use.

Bench height at edge, 16 in. to 17 in., not including cushion

OTHER WAYS TO CONFIGURE BUILT-IN DINING

Allow at least 32 in. to 36 in. between any wall cabinet and the end of the bench/edge of table.

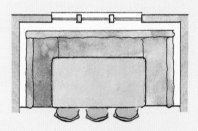

36-in. by 72-in. table with a bench on three sides

More bench seating allows for more sitters, especially if they are kid size.

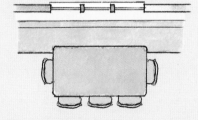

36-in. by 72-in. table with a single straight bench

This configuration is more flexible but may not fit quite as many people as the three-sided bench.

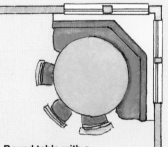

Round table with a corner bench

This configuration is both cozy and flexible. Note the angled corner; a square corner requires a square table.

•bar seating

Breakfast bars are ideal for informal dining at any time of day. Side-by-side seating may be ideal for diners who would rather read a newspaper than chat, while two-sided dining makes for more camaraderie. What people often love about bar seating is that onlookers can talk to the cook and see what's happening without getting in the way. A dining bar should be at least 18 in. deep. Bar heights range from 36 in. to 48 in. (see "Make Elbow Room for Comfortable Dining" on p. 57). It's critical to match the bar height with the height of the bar stools or chairs or vice versa. Stools are great for sliding under the countertop when not in use, but chairs add back support.

RIGHT The serious cooks in this San Francisco house love company, especially when guests are seated on the bar side of the kitchen, out of the heat of cooking. The green slate countertop shields the view of kitchen work from the living and dining spaces. The many skylights help light the kitchen during the day.

BELOW Two bar seats supplement a generous breakfast booth at left (shown on p. 59) and offer space to work on kitchen tasks while sitting down. The cantilevered stone countertop is supported by decorative wood brackets.

LEFT One of the drawbacks of bar seating is that it can be uncomfortable to sit for a long period of time. This elegant metal-trimmed foot rest takes the weight off your feet and makes it easy to linger over dinner, or work.

FACING PAGE Bar seating at an island can be as simple as cantilevering the countertop 12 in. to 15 in. over the base cabinet. The island sink is a prep sink, so no worries about dirty dishes piling up for diners to see.

ABOVE An especially deep marble countertop can handle food-prep tasks and dining or kibbutzing at the same time. The low-back bar seats tuck neatly under the countertop.

RIGHT This stone countertop cantilevers a fair amount, particularly in the center of the curve, so support is essential, especially because diners will be putting weight on it. The brackets help divvy up the bar seating, too.

Although there's a big dining table next to this new kitchen addition, bar seating is a favorite, especially with the younger set.

A door-size bifold window opens out to give diners a fresh breeze from the backyard in a dense Portland, Oregon, neighborhood. The custom bar is chair height rather than bar stool height, so it doesn't block the view from farther back in the house.

ABOVE AND RIGHT Everything radiates from this kitchen in the thick of things, with informal dining (foreground), formal dining room (background). A well-used workspace sits beside a frosted-glass door pantry and across from a big and busy bulletin board that can be hidden when company comes (right).

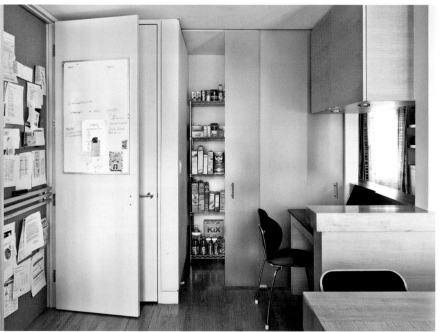

ABOVE There's a built-in desk for work or reading by the door in this country kitchen, and a comfy seat between wall ovens and microwave oven to catch up on armchair cookery. Drawers under the seat offer additional kitchen storage.

RIGHT A kitchen addition is finished off at the entry to the backyard with two comfy and useful built-in benches.

cabinets

• • •

YOU'LL LIKELY SPEND MORE TIME THINKING ABOUT CABINETS THAN any other kitchen element, and that's because cabinets are big players in the kitchen. Cabinets are the style setters, space shapers, and prime containers of our stuff. Naturally, cabinets demand a big share of the budget, too, so it's worth taking time to study cabinet choices in detail. Cabinet style, configuration, and construction details can influence almost every other kitchen component from flooring to lighting, so make cabinet decisions as early as possible. Custom or semi-custom cabinets can take a long time to make, and even the stock cabinet of your choice may not be ready to pluck off the shelf. As a rule, cabinets go in before just about everything— appliances, countertops, backsplashes, sinks, and lighting. Flooring is most often installed first and even finished, so it must be protected during cabinet installation.

Get comfortable with cabinet lingo. Start with cabinet case construction (do you prefer a face frame or a frameless case?) and door and drawer types, learn about hardware, and then dive into the vast ocean of cabinet accessories. Get creative with configuration. You don't have to match every base cabinet with a wall cabinet. You may not want to load an outside wall with wall cabinets if they will block a great view.

Now you're ready to cabinet shop, and there are so many sources today. Cabinets can be manufactured in large or small facilities, as stock or semi-custom cabinets, or built in a local shop by a cabinetmaker. If you are of a do-it-yourself bent, look at knockdown (KD) and ready-to-assemble (RTA) cabinets.

Flipper-door frosted-glass panels let dishware colors and patterns pop, but not too much. Frameless base cabinets, flat-slab doors and drawers, and simple thumb pulls keep the kitchen looking contemporary. The veneer is African anigre.

the cabinet case: face frame or frameless?

●●● CABINETS START WITH THE BASIC BOX called the case (also called a carcase or carcass), which is either face frame or frameless. A face-frame cabinet case, the most common in the United States, obtains its strength and looks from a frame of horizontal rails and vertical stiles applied to the exposed edges of the case. Doors mount to that frame and can either fit flush into the frame or overlay all or part of the frame. Because it takes more time and care to construct components that must fit closely together, face-frame cabinets with inset doors and drawers are pricier than face-frame cabinets with overlay doors and drawers. Face-frame cabinets with partial overlay doors and drawers are less expensive than full overlay doors because there's a wider gap between doors and drawers.

A frameless cabinet case is a box with no face frame. (Frameless cabinets are also called European cabinets because the technique was born in Europe in the 1950s in response to a lack of lumber and the need for speedier construction.) Because there's no frame to add stiffness, the case itself must be built stronger than a face-frame case; ¾-in.-thick sides will make the sturdiest frameless case. From the outside, it's not always easy to tell face-frame cabinets from frameless because doors and drawers for both can be flush overlay. Open a door or drawer to look for the frame. See "What's the Difference?" on the facing page for more differences.

These overlay doors in frameless cases are lightly stained to accentuate the ash veneer. The frameless cases require vertical spacers at inside corners so that doors can open properly. The narrow reveal at the top of wall cabinets is an elegant contemporary detail that requires careful craftsmanship. The dishwasher drawers and refrigerator are covered by matching panels.

WHAT'S THE DIFFERENCE?

THE CABINET CASE

- A **face frame** can make it easier to fit cabinets into a space that isn't completely square and plumb.
- A **face-frame** cabinet has a narrower opening than a **frameless** cabinet of the same width, so pull-out shelves and drawers must be narrower.
- A **frameless** cabinet has no stile or rail in front of the contents, so it can be easier to pull out stored items; an exception is an especially wide sink cabinet that may require a center post.
- A **face-frame** cabinet gets much of its strength from the frame, whereas a **frameless** cabinet depends on a stronger, thicker back and strong corner joints.

DOORS AND DRAWERS

- In **frameless** cabinets, doors and drawers usually overlay the case completely (these are called full overlay or flush overlay); **frameless** cabinets rarely have inset doors.
- In **face-frame** cabinets, doors and drawers may overlay the frame completely, may be inset, or may overlay the frame partially (called reveal overlay or half overlay).
- Inset doors, which are the traditional standard in Colonial- and Shaker-style cabinets, can require more precision in their making and installation than overlay doors.

DOOR HARDWARE

- Concealed adjustable hinges are available for both **frameless** and **face-frame** cabinet doors. They commonly adjust in three directions and are easy to tweak over the lifetime of the cabinet.
- Inset doors, almost exclusively in **face-frame** cases, traditionally are hung with butt hinges, which require more precision to install than do adjustable hinges.

These frameless cabinets abutting the range feature oversize drawers with extra-beefy slide hardware, perfect for storing pots and pans. Drawers this wide and tall can handle a frame-and-panel face, while narrow drawers are simple flat slabs.

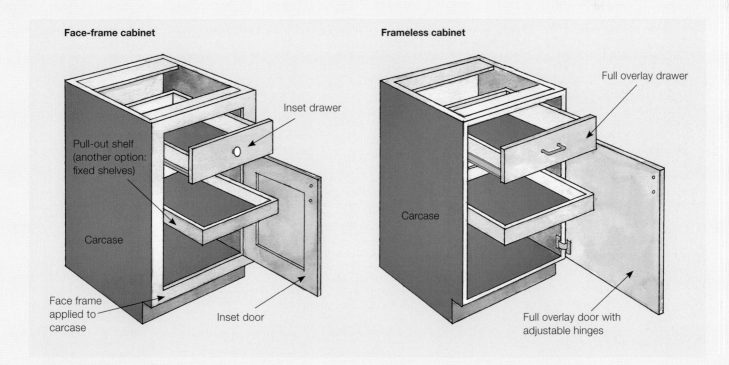

Face-frame cabinet

Inset drawer

Pull-out shelf (another option: fixed shelves)

Carcase

Face frame applied to carcase

Inset door

Frameless cabinet

Full overlay drawer

Carcase

Full overlay door with adjustable hinges

cabinet doors and drawer faces

●●● INSET DOORS AND DRAWERS, WHICH fit flush with a face frame, tend to be more costly than overlay doors because of the extra precision required. Most hinges on inset cabinets are visible, with mortised butt hinges and leaf hinges being the traditional styles.

Overlay doors and drawers affix to the surface of a face frame or the interior of a frameless case, and adjustable cup hinges allow for adjustment during installation and even years later. Full overlay doors and drawers, the standard on frameless cabinets and also used on face-frame cabinets, almost touch each other and thus take more care to build and install than reveal overlay doors and drawers, which are spaced wider apart. Reveal overlay doors and drawers (also called partial overlay) are used on face-frame cabinets.

Whether inset or overlay, doors and drawers are made in two basic types: Frame-and-panel doors and drawer faces are the more traditional style, with a frame often made of solid wood and panels that are solid or veneered medium-density fiberboard (MDF). Panels can themselves be flat, beaded, beveled, perforated or carved wood (or wood-like material), or glass (clear or patterned). Because wall cabinets are the most visible, they make good candidates for more detail and for glass panels; use clear glass for showcasing items and textured or frosted glass for a more abstracted view. Ideally, showcase cabinets can be fit up with lighting.

Flat-slab (also called one-piece) doors and drawer faces are made from glued solid wood or MDF veneered with any number of materials, most commonly wood but also plastic laminate, metal, or even glass. All-metal doors and drawers are a boon for the chemically sensitive.

RIGHT Overlay doors and drawer faces with vertical grain require precise craftsmanship and careful veneer matching. The dishwasher is covered by a matching panel.

FAR RIGHT These stock flat-frame-and-panel drawers are from IKEA. Low drawer sides offer easy access of pull-out shelves.

Japanese tansu cabinetry inspired the door and drawer face details in this cabinetmaker's kitchen. Cabinets are quartersawn beeswing sapele (akin to mahogany). The window trim and sash are Douglas fir. A wall bump-out makes room for an extra-deep countertop of honed Absolute Black granite.

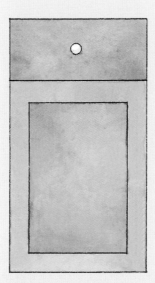

BASE CABINET DRAWER FACE AND DOOR OPTIONS

Flat-slab drawer over a frame-and-panel door with concealed hinges

A shallow drawer often looks less fussy with a flat-slab face rather than a face frame, and it will pair well with any kind of door.

Drawer in a beaded-edge frame over a beaded frame-and-raised-panel door with butt hinges

The drawer face borrows the beading detail from the door design but not the raised panel.

ABOVE These bamboo-veneer custom cabinets have frameless cases. Wall cabinet cases are thicker than the usual frameless case and are finished to be seen, some with open shelves and some covered with sliding glass doors or swinging solid doors. Base cabinet drawers are flush overlay. The countertop is concrete.

RIGHT These overlay doors flip up for full access, an especially handy design for unloading dishes from the dishwasher. The deeper lower edge conceals lighting.

the two basic categories of drawers and doors are frame and panel and flat slab (also called one-piece, but that doesn't necessarily mean monolithic). Some cabinet cases are shown as frameless and some are face frame, but be assured that either category of doors/drawers can be used in either type of cabinet case. Although door and drawer faces should be compatible, they don't need to be identical. Drawer detailing for shallow drawers looks best if it's simpler than the detailing on a door or a wide drawer. Hardware can be simpler too.

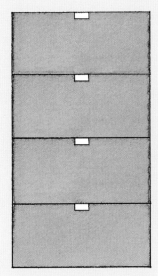

A stack of same-size flat-slab overlay drawers with finger pulls

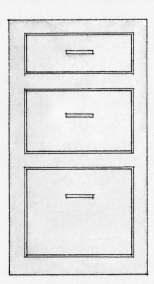

Graduated-size drawers inset in a beaded face-frame case with intermediate rails

Intermediate rails provide strength and look traditional. Beading the frame instead of the drawer is a simpler, longer-lasting detail

Graduated-size drawers inset in a face frame without intermediate rails

Eliminating the intermediate rails between drawers looks less traditional but increases cabinet capacity.

LEFT These unusual cabinets have frameless cases fitted with inset flat-slab doors and drawer faces. The wood is mahogany. Under the island countertop, the two receptacles have face plates to match.

•drawer construction

For drawers that will be doing heavy lifting of pots, pans, and dishes, look for well-built drawer boxes built with ½-in. to ¾-in. Melamine®, solid wood, or birch plywood. Shallow drawers can have sides as thin as ½ in. Metal and plastic sides can be plenty strong and are well suited to a streamlined look. Shelves that carry heavy loads should also have thick bottoms. The strongest, best-looking drawers have dovetailed corners, but corners that are doweled, screwed, or stapled are less expensive and, if built well, can do the job. A wide drawer—anything over 24 in.—works most efficiently with two knobs, two short pulls, or a long wire pull.

ABOVE Well-crafted cabinets need not be solid wood, as evidenced by this semi-custom aluminum-and-elm European cabinet drawer. Unobtrusive silverware dividers practically disappear. The countertop is engineered stone.

RIGHT African anigre veneer faces these overlay doors and drawers. Both doors and drawers are fitted with subtle thumb pulls.

DRAWER GLIDES

drawers are operated by glides, also called guides or slides. Full-extension glides allow access to the entire length of a drawer, and that convenience may outweigh the extra expense, especially for big drawers for pots and pans and shallow drawers that carry flatware; in fact, pretty much every drawer. Quiet, self-closing slides are another feature many homeowners are willing to spring for, especially in a house with enthusiastic door and drawer closers. Where a traditional look is important, or if you don't like the looks of side-mounted slides, consider undermount slides, which are more expensive than side-mounted. These take up a bit of room from the depth of the drawer, but side-mounted slides shave off a bit of the width. In any case, make sure slides are sized to serve the expected weight of drawer and contents.

ABOVE This well-made inset drawer box is built from solid wood and topped with walnut trim for contrast. Corners are dovetailed and glides are undermount. Slanted spice shelves are custom built.

hardware

● ● ● HARDWARE MAY BE A PHYSICALLY SMALL part of the kitchen cabinet package, but it has a big influence on perceived quality, so spending a little more for style and quality may be worth it. Pairing cabinets with knobs, pulls, and hinges can be tricky or not, depending on how much uniformity you prefer and if you prefer hardware to contrast or match cabinet color. One tactic for ensuring coordination is to choose a finish—brushed nickel or oil-rubbed bronze, for example—and then vary pull sizes and details with the size and function of the cabinet doors and drawers. Use wider pulls or two knobs for wide drawers and narrow pulls for narrow drawers. Finishes with the same name may not match between hardware manufacturers, so always compare samples in person. Mixing hardware finishes on a wall of cabinets can create the unfitted kitchen look, as can finishing cabinets in different colors. This option can save money because it's easier to find smaller batches of hardware in online closeout sales.

A Mediterranean-style kitchen redo features white cabinets accented by black-finished solid-brass bin pulls, cupboard turn latches, and butt hinges.

sing knobs on drawers and pulls on cabinet doors is natural because of the relative sizes of drawers and doors, but you can choose either knobs or pulls on both drawers and doors. A 1¼-in. knob is a comfortable size for standard-size drawers. A knob with a rose—the round plate at the base of the shaft—can keep a drawer looking neater because fingers are less likely to touch the drawer face. Bin pulls look cleaner longer because fingers pull from the inside, but are a little tougher to thoroughly clean than are knobs or wire pulls. Drawers over 24 in. usually require a long pull or two pulls or knobs—remember to use both to keep the drawer from eventually racking. Storing dishtowels on long drawer pulls is handy but limits access to lower drawers or doors. Knobs and pulls on drawers, which usually have a face attached to the drawer box, require longer screws than those for door hardware. Keep proportion in mind for drawer hardware: A small knob can look puny on a big drawer, and a big bin pull can look silly on a small drawer. Or forgo added knobs and pulls altogether in favor of a recessed pull or invisible catch that opens when you push on the door or drawer.

ABOVE Drawer edge pulls are sized to match drawer width, with the wider pulls allowing one- or two-handed opening. Flush-mounted ring pulls allow wide cabinet doors to slide back into the cabinet.

LEFT Salvaged and refinished bolts make bold pulls on the drawers and doors. The cabinets were shop built from reclaimed Douglas fir, and the flat frames and panels highlight the strong figure of the wood.

Identical stainless-steel thumb pulls tie together the white base cabinets, the pantry, and the refrigerator cabinetry.

HINGES

oncealed adjustable hinges, the standard for frameless cabinets, allow a cabinet door to be easily adjusted during installation and years later, often allowing the cabinet to swing completely open and out of traffic. Investigate adjustable hinges with a built-in soft closing feature if you're family is prone to slamming doors. Adjustable hinges are now available for inset doors in face-frame cabinets, too. Most cabinet doors require two hinges, but long doors such as those on a pantry may require three or more.

The more traditional hinges for inset doors are **butt hinges**, either nonmortised (surface mounted) or mortised (set into the case). Installing mortised butt hinges requires extra time and precision but creates a smooth fit between the door and the frame. If cabinet hinges aren't self-closing, **catches** may be required to keep the doors closed. Catches range from invisible rare-earth magnets, which can be inserted into both door and stile or case to hold the door shut, to knobs that you physically turn to open. Latches, which swing up to open, are traditional closers that look authentically old but take extra effort to use. A butt hinge, and its close cousin, the olive-knuckle hinge, are likely the hinge of choice on glass-door cabinets because a concealed adjustable hinge would not be hidden.

ABOVE The most elegant operating hardware for a high-quality dovetail drawer is the invisible undermount slide.

BELOW Frameless cabinets almost always are fitted with adjustable hinges, which are not only easy to adjust during installation but remain easy to adjust in the years to come.

ABOVE Base cabinet inset drawers and a flip-up appliance-garage door above are fitted with nickel pulls, and doors have matching nickel butt hinges. The doorknobs are dark oiled bronze for contrast.

cabinet accessories

● ● ● WELL-ORGANIZED CABINET SPACE IS a better investment than more cabinet space. Some accessories are static and simply divide space; others are mechanical and slide or swing out, up, or down; and some, like the lazy Susan, rotate. What all good accessories do is allow you to sort, store, and easily access your kitchen items. Accessories that are designed for your cabinets can be built in during manufacturing or in the shop or purchased as part of a stock or semi-stock cabinet package. Consider built-in vertical slots for flat items such as trays, cookie sheets, and cutting boards, and deep slots for storing wine bottles. If you like your coffee maker out of sight after breakfast or prefer to keep your stand mixer dust-free until baking time, the tried-and-still-true appliance garage is a good choice. Go for a lift-up, tilt-in, or swing door rather than the more problematic tambour door. Pull-out shelves can handle small appliances, too. A spring-up shelf allows you to store a mixer or other heavy appliance under the counter until you need it.

If you have the energy and the time, you are likely to save money by delving into the many after-market accessories available online and in home-furnishing and big-box stores. In fact, refitting existing cabinets with off-the-shelf cabinet accessories can give a tired kitchen a big boost of energy.

Extra-deep, -wide, and -strong drawers are comfortable for everyone. These are in a handy location near the dishwasher, close to the cooktop and directly under the countertop where plates are set out for serving dinner. Dishes are held in place by adjustable wood dividers.

RIGHT An appliance garage both stores appliances and conceals receptacles, so it's ideal for keeping a small urban kitchen looking neat and organized. Sliding garage doors don't infringe on precious countertop space.

BELOW Custom-made pull-out shelves in a Seattle kitchen redo bring spice jars and cans close to the cooktop and food-prep space but not so close as to overheat them.

ABOVE Custom-made Arts and Crafts–style cabinetry includes a split drawer that divides for double-duty. The top section is a pull-out prep space, and the bottom is a drawer for cutting board storage. The matte black countertop is PaperStone®.

drawers versus pull-out shelves

Once upon a time, the only storage option in a base cabinet was a fixed shelf. Then pull-out shelves came along to make it easier to see cabinet contents. With the invention of heavy-duty glide hardware, the traditional drawer has grown large enough to handle items that once were hung on hooks or stashed on shelves in base cabinets. Now one of the first questions to answer in a kitchen project is, Do you want all drawers in your base cabinets or a combination of pull-out shelves and drawers?

Pull-out shelves have low sides and fronts that excel at allowing a side view, which is handy for a quick ID of jars, cans, and bottles. The low sides also allow for handles and other bits to stick up and out, unlike drawers, so you may find they hold more than drawers. Pull-out shelves can usually be adjusted to suit the containers you want to store. On the other hand, because pull-out shelf walls aren't as high as those of a drawer, things can fall out; a drawer is better at corralling its contents. A major advantage of a drawer is that it takes one motion to see inside whereas you have to open a cabinet door, then tug on the pull-out shelf. But one version of the base cabinet with pull-outs has a stack of low shelves attached directly to a cabinet door panel that glides straight out with one motion. Overall, a base cabinet full of drawers will be more expensive than a base cabinet with drawers on the top row and doors with pull-out shelves on the bottom.

This built-in cabinet has both fixed and pull-out shelves. At low and mid-range height, the pull-out shelves are easy to see and access, while the fixed shelves are a more comfortable choice for the upper reaches of the cabinet.

RIGHT This custom-made base cabinet offers three layers of roll-out cabinetry. The shelf on top is supported by heavy-duty drawer glides and is clad with a stainless-steel appliance panel to handle straight-from-the-oven pots. The two drawers below offer space for other kitchen gear. The cabinets are quartersawn beeswing sapele, and the countertop is honed Absolute Black granite.

BELOW Double-decker pull-out shelves to the right of the range offer a clear view of the contents. Unlike individual pull-out shelves, which require you to first open a door, this design offers one-step access.

BELOW A stand-alone cooktop won't generate heat like an oven, so it makes sense to store spices and condiments in the adjacent base cabinet. A solid back panel provides structural support, and shelves are shallow enough for easy viewing from one side.

Door-mounted shelves and swing-out hardware are easy to reach, and they move out of the way for getting to storage deep in the corner, usually the dark abyss of kitchen cabinetry.

RIGHT The pull-out shelf accessory requires a two-handed operation—open door, pull out shelf—but these shelves hold a lot of gear and are easy to survey with a quick glance.

blind cabinet corners are a challenge to budgets, ingenuity, and patience. Look for a lazy Susan without a center post for more flexible storage or one with wire shelves for better visibility. Complex, swing-out and pull-out racks allow full access but do remember that the more moving parts, the more expensive. Wall cabinets have corners, too, but aren't as hard to access because of their shallow depth. Fitting up corners in wall cabinets with well-lit open shelving can solve access problems and make a kitchen seem more spacious. As you contemplate corner cabinets, make sure there's room for doors and drawers to open fully. Another option is to avoid corner cabinetry altogether.

The extreme curve in this end cabinet allows for easier comings and goings in a renovated old-house kitchen, and it still allows space for a drawer. Aftermarket accessories make good use of the drawer space.

sizing and configuring cabinets from top to bottom

● ● ● AS YOU LAY OUT YOUR KITCHEN, IT'S natural to visualize cabinets side by side, but take the time to look up and down to consider how cabinets look, and study elevations to make sure that cabinets fit your work style from top to bottom. The standard cabinet types are base cabinets and wall cabinets, but you don't have to stop there. The floor-to-ceiling cabinet, such as a china cabinet, offers loads of storage, and if it's positioned at a transitional spot, say, between kitchen and mudroom or kitchen and dining, it can really shape the space and offer a place to show off dishware and other decorative items. Don't worry about getting wall cabinets to line up with base cabinets perfectly. Appliances, windows, and other visual elements throw off upper and lower cabinet alignment, and in any case the backsplash provides a visual break. An exception might be a prominently placed china cabinet, which is an all-of-a-piece element.

A full-depth, floor-to-ceiling cabinet acts as a pantry, while the more standard base cabinet and wall cabinet combo provides uncommonly sleek storage for dishware. The orange solid-surface waterfall countertop makes a brilliant end panel.

ABOVE Solid-door transom cabinets provide hidden storage for less-used items, and a hefty crown molding covers the gap between cabinetry and ceiling.

RIGHT A sink cabinet is distinguished from its neighbors by elaborate feet and by a unique configuration of drawers and panels.

t he standard base cabinet is just shy of 2 ft. deep and usually 34½ in. tall to allow for a 1½-in. countertop, ending up at 36 in. above the floor. If you want to vary either the depth or the height of the countertop, it's possible to specify taller or deeper cabinets. But there are less expensive ways to make countertops taller and deeper. For more height, set a standard case on a taller base. For more countertop depth, have standard cabinets installed several inches from the wall, and make sure that any end gap is covered with wide matching panel.

It's tough to reach items stored up high, so it makes sense to designate top shelves for well-lit decorative display, as seen in these taller-than-standard cabinets. The single door has two panels; the glass in the upper panel is a less-expensive alternative to stacked wall cabinets.

m o r e   a b o u t . . .
STACKED/TRANSOM WALL CABINETS

the stacked (two-level) wall cabinet is an elegant fashion favorite. The top cabinet, sometimes called a transom cabinet, is often glazed and lit from within, and while it's too high for everyday storage, it's ideal for showcasing favorite objects. Transom cabinets with solid doors are good for storing less-used items. A less-expensive way to achieve the stacked wall cabinet look is to design a wall cabinet look-alike. Inset a square panel of glass in the cabinet door tops, set top shelves at the right height for display, and add interior lighting.

UNIVE
DETAI

niversal desi
geared to ma
for people of all age
make your cabinets
consider these detai

• Choose full-extens
  drawers and pull-o
• Make use of acces
  out, rotate, or swir
  for corner cabinet
• Locate wall cabine
  or simply leave off
  store most items in
  base cabinets.

In this extra-tall kitchen
space, the high pantry
cabinet is detailed
like a freestanding
armoire, but with a
contemporary flat top.

tandard wall cabinets are 30 in. high; if set at the suggested 15 in. to 18 in. above a standard 36-in.-high countertop, they won't reach the ceiling. You could allocate extra space above standard-height wall cabinets for display, tuck lighting behind cornice molding to add ambience, or drop the ceiling to make a soffit for lighting or ductwork. But today it's more popular to take cabinets to the ceiling, either by installing the wall cabinets higher or ordering taller cabinets and filling any gap with molding. For taller wall cabinets, make sure opened doors will clear light fixtures and be sure sufficient space remains for trim to fit between the door and the ceiling; an elaborate crown molding requires more space, of course. While trim eases the visual and physical transition between cabinet and ceiling, trimless contemporary-style cabinets may simply touch the ceiling or be set off by a narrow reveal. Both details demand an exceptionally flat ceiling for the best effect.

Base cabinets sit on solid bases or on legs, which can be exposed or covered by solid trim. A common detail is to design the base recessed in front to create a toe space. Stock face-frame and many frameless manufactured cabinets have a 4-in.-high, 3-in.-deep toe space. European-style cabinets more often have tall toe spaces, from 5 in. to 8 in. Toe spaces can be fitted up to store step stools, trays, or the family silver. The toe space is also ideal for locating the supply register. The unfitted cabinet style, with added legs to look more like furniture, is a variation on the simple toe space. Some island cabinets are designed to rest on plinths that project from the case; this detail requires a deeper countertop so that you stand farther from the cabinet and don't bump the plinth with your toes.

abinet sizes and c
depend on the sp
appliances you select, sc
you want appliances to w
the appliance be hidden?
the cabinetry? Should it
operation? Appliance do
cabinet doors and drawe
For example, a dishwash
can keep a drawer from

materials and finishes

●●● CABINET INTERIORS DO THE GRUNT work, while exteriors do the dazzling. Most cabinets are wood, whether solid or veneered onto cabinet cases, doors, and drawers, and most manufacturers and cabinet shops offer an exciting variety of wood species and finishes. Solid wood sounds good, but it's touchier in moist climates than is wood veneered on a sturdy panel product like high-quality plywood. If historic style is a factor, think quartersawn oak, cherry, Douglas fir, pine, hickory, chestnut, or maple. These species can also look fine with modern detailing, with less traditional species like various types of mahogany, bamboo, and zebrawood appearing most often as contemporary cabinets. Most wood cabinets are sprayed with catalyzed varnish, but for authentically old-looking cabinets, hand-applied finishes can be had for considerably more money. With any wood cabinets, proper preparation is important; no sanding marks should be visible on any quality cabinet. Hand-applied glazes and paints and high-gloss lacquer are the most costly finishes. Painted cabinets—especially those with glossy finishes—show dings more easily than clear-finished wood cabinets and may not be as easy to touch up. Door and drawer panel products (plywood or MDF) can be veneered with wood, rigid thermafoil (RTF), metal, and 21st-century plastic laminate. Stainless-steel and coated steel cabinets offer pro-style gleam and durability.

A small, highly energy-efficient house in Maine features low-maintenance, locally sourced materials, and energy-saving details. The granite for the countertop and backsplash was quarried a mere 20 miles away, and wall and base cabinets were made by a local shop. A pull-out recirculating range hood fan filters out grease and moisture but sends the heated air back into the room mixed with fresh air.

LEFT This floor-to-ceiling pantry cabinet is walnut with flat-frame-and-panel doors and flat-slab drawers.

BELOW This handsome flatware drawer with elegant dovetails has a sapele mahogany face attached to a birch plywood box.

a l o o k a t . . .

CABINET CASE MATERIALS

It's important to look beyond those pretty door and drawer faces to take note of what your cabinet cases will be made from. There's not a clear consensus about what makes the very best cabinet case. For years, the highest quality wood-based cabinet cases have been made from ¾-in. veneer-core plywood, which is stronger, lighter in weight, more resistant to moisture, and better at taking fasteners than both medium-density fiberboard (MDF) and particleboard. Some cabinetmakers prefer MDF over plywood for its dimensional stability and for a smooth face that's ideal for applying veneers and other laminates, so keep an open mind about MDF, which is usually less expensive than veneer-core plywood. There's no argument that particleboard is the least expensive and lowest-quality of case goods but it's also the most commonly used case material in manufactured cabinets.

If your budget allows, choose plywood for cabinets where water could potentially cause damage. For dry locations, look to MDF or even particleboard, but also consider the recent plywood mash-up, combi-core. Combi-core plywood retains the strong and light veneer plywood core but is sandwiched between layers of MDF to provide a smooth, stable surface.

Case interiors can be painted; veneered with plastic laminate or wood (maple and beech are popular); or more economically finished with vinyl, foil, or paper films. Melamine thermofused onto particleboard makes a case with a ready-made, easy-to-clean surface. Melamine can be white, black, or patterned to look like wood and is less expensive than wood veneer but more durable than paint or film. Most wood or wood-veneered cabinets are finished in the shop or at least primed if they are paint grade.

•cabinet sources

Cabinet sources range widely, and in fact, cabinet components themselves are likely to come from various sources. Even custom cabinetmakers may shop out components to specialized sources and then assemble the components in their own shops. Stock and semi-custom cabinets increasingly come from one of the many cabinet manufacturers that purchase cabinet parts from companies that specialize in doors, drawers, or cases. That's not a bad thing if the components are well made and reliable. In fact, you can mix and match yourself. You may want to source custom or semi-custom cabinets for high-visibility locations, such as the island, and use stock or DIY cabinets for perimeter locations. No matter the cabinet source, take time to study carefully the plans, shop drawings, specifications and lists of hardware, accessories, and/or cabinet components.

LEFT These semi-custom cabinets fit a renovated kitchen like a glove, with details such as transom cabinets at the top for display and massive drawers for storing pots and pans.

CUSTOM
CABINETS

ustom cabinets crafted in a cabinetmaker's shop aren't necessarily the most expensive but they can be, and their fabrication often takes longer than semi-custom cabinets. A cabinetmaker may not necessarily be building your cabinets from scratch but may combine components from several specialized sources with shop-built cases. If the components are made well—and computers are helping people make straighter and squarer cabinet components—this way of cabinetmaking can result in both a shorter lead time and a higher-quality product. And it may be a less-expensive alternative to higher-end semi-custom cabinetry, so do check out local cabinet shops. Always ask a cabinetmaker for references, and always take the time to see the referenced cabinetry in person.

ABOVE This custom cabinetry was designed in conjunction with the architecture of the kitchen, with small windows placed behind the two high display shelves. To give the wall cabinets a truly built-in look, glass-door transom cabinets are topped with a fully integrated soffit and finished with crown molding.

STOCK AND SEMI-CUSTOM MANUFACTURED CABINETS

Stock cabinets can be bought off the shelf or ordered from a big-box store, home center, or lumberyard or through a kitchen products dealer, designer, or contractor, with installation available for an additional fee. As a general rule, stock cabinets are built as individual components in standard sizes and in 3-in. increments, so if a run of cabinets isn't quite as wide as the space you are looking to fill, stock filler pieces will span the gaps. Or, for a more custom look, cover gaps and embellish corners and augment wall cabinet tops with cornices purchased from decorative molding suppliers. Stock cabinets these days can come in a dizzying variety of finishes, colors, styles, and sizes and still tend to be about half the cost of many semi-custom and custom cabinets.

Semi-custom cabinets are also manufactured (as opposed to shopmade), but they are made to order for a specific project and from a wider range of styles, finishes, hardware, accessories, sizes, and configurations than are stock cabinets. Cabinets can be built as larger assemblies rather than simply case by case. Semi-custom cabinetry tends to be higher quality and higher priced than stock cabinets, sometimes by a considerable amount.

BELOW AND FACING PAGE, BOTTOM This kitchen had been poorly laid out but the cabinets were in excellent shape, so cabinet cases were moved, one major cabinet interior was completely reworked, and old cabinets were refaced to match new ones. Formerly a wall oven cabinet, the tall pantry cabinet (shown on the facing page) is now fit up with a big drawer, pull-out shelves, and fixed shelves. The cabinets are Douglas fir with Craftsman details; the countertop is PaperStone.

RIGHT Semi-custom and custom cabinets are often fit up with handsome wood dividers for keeping kitchen tools tidy; they can be designed to suit a homeowner's particular cooking needs.

DO-IT-YOURSELF CABINETRY

f you're handy, consider going the DIY route with knockdown (KD) cabinets or ready-to-assemble (RTA) cabinets. KD and RTA cabinets are factory manufactured and finished components that are shipped with all parts, fasteners, and instructions packaged together. Holes are predrilled and sometimes dowels are preglued. The intent is that specialized power tools aren't required for assembling these cabinets, making them a viable and less-expensive option for anyone who's fairly handy and patient. Buying stock cabinets off the shelf in person will cost less than if cabinet components are shipped. Search for both KD and RTA sources online (see Resources on p. 214). Beware of KD and RTA cabinets imported from new and untried sources.

The term RTA sometimes applies to cabinet components that are sold to the trade or to serious amateur woodworkers who can speak the lingo. These may require the use of specialized tools, so read the fine print. With careful research, design, planning, and follow through, an especially intrepid homeowner may want to order cabinet components from one company that specializes in KD/RTA cases and another that specializes in doors and drawers. KD and RTA components can be ordered finished or not or mixed, with finished drawers and unfinished cases, for example. Another DIY tactic is to order cabinets unfinished and finish them yourself, but be aware that your at-home finish simply can't be as tough and uniform as a factory finish. But hand-applied paint or stain might be exactly what you are looking for.

open shelves and pantries

CABINETS MAY SQUIRREL AWAY MOST OF OUR KITCHEN GEAR, BUT there's a lot to be said about open shelving, whether it's out in the open or in a pantry. Open shelving in the kitchen proper is a more streamlined alternative to bulky wall cabinets and can make the room seem more spacious. Open shelves can also be a more economical substitute for additional wall cabinets.

The open shelf is a show-off, but in a good way. It's a pleasure to see rows of spice jars, stacks of plates, and in the pantry, a row of cereal boxes and neatly stacked paper towels. It warms the heart to see much-loved kitchen gear on display and to verify that supplies are at the ready in advance of a snowstorm or a pack of hungry teenagers. Open shelves make it easier for both cook and guests to locate cooking tools and vessels. Gear that's visible can also be an incentive to keep things tidy. If you live where dust builds up quickly, you may want to store only frequently used items on open shelves or be prepared to do some touching up on a regular basis.

What if you prefer keeping some things out of sight but not out of mind? This is where the pantry fits in, and why it came out of retirement not too long ago. A pantry is well worth its footprint, whether built into kitchen cabinetry or surrounded by three walls and a door. Open shelving in a pantry offers the same easy access without the dust and grease that can gather while sitting out in the kitchen proper. And shelving doesn't have to be as fancy as in the kitchen. Shelving in the butler's pantry, the traditional transition between kitchen and dining, can be more elegant than the kitchen.

This sunny kitchen is all about open shelving. Shelves are fixed, which makes them stiffer and more resistant to sagging than adjustable shelves. Varied shelf spacing fits items of different heights. Baskets on island shelves offer easy storage but keep clutter to a minimum.

open shelves

● ● ● OPEN SHELVES CAN GO ANYWHERE AND be any size. Tuck slim shelves in a recess between studs or attach them to the backsplash, below wall cabinets. For convenience, locate shallow shelves for frequently used and replenished spices near the cooktop or prep countertop. Fit in narrow but sturdy shelves for cooking oils and containers for holding wooden spoons and other cooking utensils. Recessed shelves should be fit only into interior walls where there's no insulation to worry about. Before cutting into existing walls, always make exploratory holes to determine if utilities are running in the wall.

Any shelves over countertops must be sized to allow you to work comfortably. Shelves lower than 15 in. to 18 in. above the countertop should be no deeper than 12 in. As with wall cabinets, the underside of an open shelf can be fit up with task lighting. Trim the front to conceal the fixture.

Fit open shelves between runs of closed wall cabinets, particularly at corners, where displayed items can be a focal point. Add shelves at the end of an island or peninsula for cookbooks and oversize kitchen items, such as salad bowls and trays.

@ s a rule of thumb, for storing or displaying objects you use often, keep the shelf almost as narrow as the objects. That way, there's no possibility of stacking objects in front. To make do with deep shelves, purchase long, skinny after-market containers to store decanted grains or corral small like items such as food-processor attachments. Rectangular containers save space. To avoid stacking items uncomfortably high, space shelves closer together to make dishes or cookware easier to retrieve. Store like items together for easier retrieval, and label decanted goods with a china marker or a nonpermanent marker. Shelves for decorative objects can be more generous in depth and spacing.

ABOVE In lieu of bulky wall cabinets, open shelves do the lifting and keep a small kitchen bright and open. Shelves rest on adjustable aluminum brackets that cantilever from standards attached to the wall. A utensil rail carries lighter loads.

RIGHT A bank of streamlined frameless cabinetry conceals a refrigerator and freezer at right and pantry shelving at left. The dark-toned interior creates an elegant, low-key look.

FACING PAGE A dark ranch house redo commenced with tearing down the wall between kitchen and dining and building dividing bookcases backed with slightly lower kitchen cabinets. The new bamboo-veneered kitchen island has its own open shelves in two heights.

•shelf materials and support

Shelf material and sizing depends on aesthetics, budget, and the span required. Solid wood and panel products can look either traditional or modern, while glass shelves tend to look contemporary. You may think of glass as being clear, but most shelf glass has a green tint. If you prefer a more colorless glass, look for low-iron glass. Wire shelves are a much more utilitarian option, and restaurant-quality wire shelving can re-create the high-functioning gleam of a restaurant kitchen.

Solid-wood shelves can be detailed to look modern, especially if the supports are hidden or sparing, but solid wood is also the most traditional shelf material, whether painted or natural. Solid wood is relatively strong, but it can warp, and it shrinks and expands with changes in humidity. Veneered plywood makes a shelf that's not only more stable than solid wood but can pass for solid wood if its edges are covered with a glue-on or iron-on edging or with an edge-band (which has the benefit of increasing the strength of the shelf). MDF and particleboard can't span as far as solid wood or plywood shelves of the same thickness and depth but can make serviceable shelves if supports are closer together to prevent sagging.

ABOVE These open shelves add color and texture by way of displayed objects and paint on the back surface, with chalkboard paint at the backsplash.

RIGHT Open shelving doesn't have to be horizontal. Open dish slots in this Brooklyn brownstone redo act both as a dish drain and storage because dishes stay here until they are used again.

This traditional Scandinavian-inspired kitchen is finished off at the ceiling with a display shelf of varying depths, with curvy brackets supporting deep shelves and a simple cleat elsewhere.

MAKE SHELVES STRONGER

here are ways to strengthen a shelf and effectively increase the load it can carry:

- Keep spans shorter. An increase in span of just 25% results in twice as much deflection.
- Add intermediate shelf supports.
- Fixed shelves are stronger than adjustable shelves and thus can have longer spans (and there's no need to drill a string of holes on each side of a cabinet).
- To greatly increase the load a shelf can support and the distance it can span between brackets, add a cleat—a narrow board or molding—continuously below the shelf, against the wall.
- To increase visual heft and add considerable stiffness to a shelf, apply a wood edge-band (a 1½-in. edge-band is common) to the front edge.

- Double the thickness of the shelf by fastening two boards together and finishing the front edge with an edge-band that covers the joint.
- Build a torsion box. This thick shelf is similar to a hollow-core door, with a honeycomb structure or plywood strips faced with two plywood skins.

Ends of islands are often prime spots for display shelving. These adjustable shelves have a deep edge-band to give them more substance.

pantries

●●● WHAT MAKES A PANTRY? SHELVES, AND lots of them. Where these shelves go is another matter. A pantry can either be crafted as cabinetry or built into the house structure, with stud walls and drywall. Each type has its advantage. A cabinet pantry can be placed close to the action and can blend in with other cabinetry for a more streamlined look, whereas the reach-in or walk-in pantry has the advantage of having everything on display at the opening of a single door. The butler's pantry is another creature altogether and is meant for looks as well as specific storage of glassware and plates, not stacks of paper towels and cereal boxes.

A pantry will be handiest if it's close to where you need it. Locate an all-dish pantry between the dishwasher and the serving countertop. If your kitchen pantry can't hold all your bulk-buy purchases, consider storing backup goods somewhere else, perhaps in the basement or in a secondary pantry near where you bring in the groceries. Keep precious kitchen space for a smaller pantry for more immediate use, then restock from the remote pantry. If possible, locate a built-in pantry closet on a cool exterior wall on the north or east side of the house.

A sunlit pantry to the right makes a cheery second workspace. The pantry is home to pots, pans, foodstuff, and small appliances, which can be hidden by a curtain. In the kitchen itself, open shelves with ornate brackets hold everyday items and bulky pieces, while most dishware is covered by glass doors with frames so slim that cabinets look open.

abinet-style pantries themselves come in many configurations. Pantry cabinets can be continuous from top to bottom, with wall and base cabinets the same depth, or the cabinet pantry can look like a china cabinet, with a smaller top cabinet placed on a deep base cabinet. Doors can be full height just on the higher cabinet, with drawers on the bottom. Shelves can be fixed or pull out. Another cabinet style is the tall, narrow roll-out unit with a stack of closely spaced fixed shelves. The inside of the cabinet doors can be fit up with narrow shelves for quick access to spices and the like. As with all cabinetry, the more complex the hardware and accessories, the higher the price. One way to cut costs is to keep pantry storage straightforward and do your own customizing by purchasing modular aftermarket dividers and other accessories.

ABOVE This built-in cabinet takes on the appearance of a free-standing china cabinet, with curvy feet at the toe space and crown molding at the top.

RIGHT An urban kitchen makes good use of little space with narrow pull-out pantry units. This custom cabinetry is mahogany.

This dish pantry is positioned near both the dishwasher and the island serving space, and it creates an elegant end cabinet to the kitchen.

WALK-IN AND REACH-IN PANTRIES

or walk-in pantries and reach-in pantries, install a variety of shelf depths. Provide shallower shelving (4 in. to 12 in.) that allows you to see and store cans, jars, bottles, and the like. Provide 18-in. to 20-in. shelving lower down, perhaps under a work counter, for bulky items. Door width is important. If the pantry is a shallow but wide reach-in, two doors are ideal, as one wide door will swing too far out, and a single, narrow door won't allow easy access. If space is tight, a pocket door can improve circulation. A louvered door helps with ventilation.

Adjustable shelves or freestanding shelving kits will make it easy to change the configuration over the years (or during the first days of fitting out your new pantry), but if you know what you want and where, fixed shelves will do fine, especially if you like a more traditional look. Solid shelves look especially traditional with brackets. But wire shelves can offer better

visibility and ventilation and can be less inviting to pantry critters. Baskets work well for corralling small items—potatoes, onions, bags of chips—and are easy to take out and put back. A pantry countertop can provide space to store and use small appliances or to cool (or hide) just-baked cookies. A stack of skinny, deep shelves can hold big but flat items such as baking pans, trays, and sheets of parchment paper.

It's best not to cover the entire wall of a walk-in pantry with shelves. Leave some room for hooks for aprons, barbecue tools, a broom, the vacuum, and perhaps space for a message board. You may want to locate recycling bins in a larger walk-in pantry, especially if it's near the back door. If you like cool pantry storage for dry goods, a walk-in pantry may not be the best place for a heat-producing appliance like a refrigerator, and it should not share space with laundry appliances.

RIGHT This tall pantry is located at the end of a run of cabinets to keep from interrupting countertop space and to allow non-cooks access without interfering with cooking. Two full-height doors make it easy to see the whole pantry. Pull-out shelves and stationary shelves are all adjustable.

ABOVE Low, adjustable pull-out shelves behind two tall doors make for easy-to-see and easy-to-access food storage.

LEFT Glass doors give this pantry space added class. Restaurant-style metal shelving keeps the pantry looking clean and bright.

ABOVE This user-friendly pantry between the mudroom/back entry and the kitchen is where groceries get dropped off and recyclables are managed. Ample countertop space for unloading bags can become a workspace for baking. The pass-through offers a shortcut for dinner ingredients.

LEFT The pantry space at the left is a vital addition in a major kitchen overhaul. The space beyond includes a desk and bookshelves. The cutouts make it easy to hand beverages and food to family members in the basement rec room.

ABOVE LEFT The best cabinet lighting is inside, where nothing interrupts the light. It's not just walk-in or reach-in pantries that have room for lighting, as this cabinet pantry shows. This fixture turns on and off via a door-operated switch.

ABOVE RIGHT Sliding doors don't interfere with circulation but do offer a half-at-a-time view of pantry contents in a tiny cottage for a retired couple who are avid cooks. Metro-style shelving makes for light, moveable, and professional-looking storage inside the pantry and in the microwave niche.

more about...
LIGHTING A PANTRY

lighting a pantry is essential. Looks don't count here, but heat does, so a simple fluorescent fixture over the door on the inside stays cool and allows light to shine on the shelves. Consider a door-operated switch or motion detector so you don't forget to turn off the light. You may want to include a charging station in the pantry, and a countertop for small appliances. Include receptacles for these gadgets, but first check local codes for any special requirements.

LEFT This hall between kitchen and dining contains a butler's pantry at left and a working pantry at right. Textured glass in the door keeps the space bright without revealing contents.

BELOW A butler's pantry just off the kitchen proper contains a small bar sink, undercabinet fridge, and storage for wineglasses. Transom cabinets at top hold seasonal glassware.

more about...
THE BUTLER'S PANTRY

u nlike the everyday pantry, a butler's pantry is no beast of burden. It's usually a passageway between kitchen and dining room, with cabinets meant for storing and displaying dishes and glassware, and is often detailed in a more formal, elegant way than the kitchen itself. The butler's pantry requires a countertop for serving plates and to act as a buffet, and it may be home to a small sink, a second dishwasher, a microwave oven, or a warming oven. A butler's pantry can offer secondary food-prep space, too, especially when multiple cooks are at work.

Shallow shelves built into the back of cabinet doors improve accessibility in two ways. The first is by making a home for smaller items that could get lost in a deep cabinet, and the second is by making the interior shelves shallower so it's easier to see everything being stored.

countertops, backsplashes, and sinks

6

• • •

COUNTERTOPS TAKE THE BRUNT OF DAILY KITCHEN WORK, BUT we still expect them to look fabulous. The ideal countertop is smooth, nonporous, nonstaining, heatproof, durable, easy to clean, resistant to scratching, handsome, and inexpensive. In real life, you'll likely need to compromise here and there to find your ideal countertop.

A backsplash at a workspace must resist food stains and water, and if it's behind the cooktop, it must hold up against a certain amount of heat. But if it's not in the line of fire, the backsplash can be the perfect canvas for showcase materials that aren't tough enough for a countertop. On the other hand, that same visual prominence can allow a simple, neutral backsplash to have a calming visual presence.

For economy and practicality, and for variety, why not tailor countertops and backsplashes to suit different kitchen tasks? Marble can provide a cool, hard surface for rolling or kneading dough, and stainless steel can make a sanitary, heatproof prep zone and landing space alongside a cooktop. A glazed tile or stainless-steel backsplash makes a great backdrop for cooking or food prep. A beadboard backsplash may not suit a heavy-duty cooking zone but would be a handsome surface in a less active kitchen zone.

The demand for good looks and performance applies to sinks and faucets too, whether work, prep, or bar sink. You'll spend a lot of time standing at a sink, so make it comfortable for your height and work habits. Test various sizes and set-ups as you shop, and consider faucet and other sink fittings.

A single-bowl enameled cast iron sink is deep enough for splash-free vegetable washing and has room for soaking baking sheets. The green granite countertop accommodates a faucet, its single handle, and a purified hot water dispenser. The backsplash is glazed ceramic tile.

textures and finishes

●●● IT'S POSSIBLE TO MAKE YOUR COUNTERTOP and backsplash a perfect match, but these days you'll often see countertop and backsplash materials complement or contrast each other. Color, finish, and materials can mix and match to suit function, budget, and aesthetics.

The ideal countertop finish depends on kitchen habits and expectations. A leathered stone surface may be easier to keep looking clean than highly polished stone, depending on the particular type of stone and the particular finish. Irregular textures can suit the backsplash, although a rough surface might not be ideal behind an active cooktop because it's tough to clean nooks and crannies, even with sealed stone. Keep in mind that glossy surfaces show scratches and smudges more prominently. The exception to this rule is that some honed stones will show smudges more readily. If small scratches on a countertop will drive you nuts, you'll want to make cutting boards mandatory, no matter what the countertop material. Also be aware that a glossy backsplash or countertop will reflect undercabinet lighting and even the undercabinet surface, warts and all.

The best bet is for you to check out countertop materials and finish textures in action before you buy. And be aware that of all kitchen finishes, countertops and backsplashes are the most emotionally charged. You may well feel buyer's remorse the day after you place the order and the day after installation. Be patient, and chances are you will grow to love your choices.

Universal design tips: Honed stone is easier on the eyes, and an edge contrast helps define the counter edge, making it easier to keep things on the counter.

Tradition meets the 21st century in a New England countryside kitchen. A generous sink fabricated from soapstone slabs is the centerpiece of a big island, while the big range opposite is backed by stainless steel. The contemporary single-handled faucet is an ergonomic choice for a big family.

ABOVE This farm-style kitchen is fit up with both soapstone countertops and IKEA butcher-block countertops. Soapstone makes a tough but handsome windowsill too. Painted beadboard serves as a sturdy backsplash behind the butcher-block.

BELOW There are no backsplashes in this contemporary kitchen, only windows to a lovely natural view. On the island, a slightly higher countertop defines the edge of the wash-up space and calls out the perimeter of the dining surface.

more about...
COUNTERTOP SIZING

llot the right amount of space for countertops. Most appliances require a 15-in. landing space on one or both sides, while each of the kitchen's cooks need a 36-in.-wide space for food preparation. While 36-in.-high countertops are standard, you may prefer some countertops at different heights. For most kitchen tasks, a comfortable height is 4 in. to 6 in. below the bent elbow, but some tasks, like kneading dough and rolling pastry, are more comfortable on a lower surface. If you crave deeper countertops but not the price of custom-size base cabinets, have base cabinets installed a few inches from the wall. Cover any exposed sides with deeper panels to hide the gap.

LEFT White and ebony create a bright and stylish kitchen in a space that used to be three small, dark rooms. Countertops and backsplashes are Carrara marble; cabinets are face frame with flat-frame-and-panel Craftsman-style doors. Oil-rubbed bronze hardware picks up on the deep richness of the ebony-stained wood floor.

ABOVE A lowered pastry workstation is topped with honed marble and finished with a polished marble backsplash. Soapstone countertops with low backsplashes are topped with painted beadboard.

more about...
BACKSPLASH ALTERNATIVES

or the most complete resistance to stains and water, fill the entire space between countertop and cabinet bottom with backsplash material. But what if that's too expensive? The standard 4-in. plastic laminate cove backsplash is good enough, but consider easy-to-clean satin or glossy paint or water-resistant wallpaper instead. A 6-in.- to 12-in.-high decorative tile border or a 4-in. to 8-in. painted or stained wood molding can be topped off with paint or wallpaper. This can be a fine backsplash for a less messy workspace, especially where there are no wall cabinets and it's too pricey to cover the whole wall with stone or tile.

ABOVE Honed marble countertops are topped with sparkling tile backsplashes, and the center island is topped with 3-in. edge-grain maple butcher-block. Pendants have vintage mercury glass shades. Drawer pulls are polished nickel.

LEFT In a small home in the woods, a kitchen is open to living space and to dining (built-in benches and a big table are center left), so finishes are elegant. A broad green granite countertop serves as prep surface, landing space for the wall oven and microwave ovens below, and offers an informal dining counter. Cabinetry is mahogany veneer.

A white backsplash and white countertop keep this tiny city kitchen looking serene, while the texture of glass mosaic tile and gentle figure of Carrara marble add understated detail. The sink is especially wide and deep but it's slightly narrow back to front to allow a broad band of marble to span the front edge.

COUNTERTOP AND BACKSPLASH MATERIALS

With today's burgeoning marketplace of countertop and backsplash materials, making decisions about which countertop goes with which backsplash can be agonizing. Borrow or even purchase the largest samples you can and live with them a while. Do backsplash and countertop complement or clash?

Consider durability, ease of maintenance, looks, surface feel, and, of course, cost. Some countertop and backsplash materials can be installed only by licensed fabricators and some are DIY friendly. And look at how green a countertop is with the understanding that this is a complex issue. Where do the materials come from, how are they made, are they safe for your household, will they stand up to use? Many factors go into determining whether a material is environmentally friendly, including transportation, content and origin of raw materials, manufacturing processes, and renewability. Stone may be quarried close to you, but is it finished nearby or does it travel overseas for finishing? Can backsplash and countertops be recycled if you tire of them? (See Resources on p. 214 for more information.)

Although square footage estimates can be a start for determining costs, the design of your countertop will have a big impact on the budget, too. Consider such factors as the breadth and width of countertops, seam locations, edge profiles, sink and faucet cutouts, and if base cabinets need to be beefier to support heavy loads.

If you're tempted to install your own countertops, look at tile, wood, plastic laminate, and composite paper, as these can be worked on-site, after research and with diligence. Most other countertop materials are prepared off-site with small adjustments and cutouts handled on-site by experienced craftspeople, and some materials, such as solid surfacing and engineered stone, require installation by an installer certified by the manufacturer.

ABOVE A kitchen for multiple cooks and diners has a big butcher-block countertop that can be converted from prep to dining space. Perimeter counters are honed black granite. Glossy subway tile covers the low backsplash and header space over the windows.

LEFT This sink cabinet and the black granite countertop bump out a bit to embrace the farmhouse sink and to make room for a soap dispenser, single-lever faucet, sprayer, and filtered water dispenser.

SOLID WOOD AND BAMBOO

kitchen surfaces made of wood have been around for centuries—we call them tables. Wood makes a serviceable and beautiful countertop, as it's soft and warm in tone, soft to the touch, quiet, and easy on dishes. It helps if you feel comfortable with wood developing a patina, and if you care for it properly. Wood can survive some heat, but it can still get scorched or stained by a hot or wet cast-iron pan. Drying up spills immediately is essential to maintain a wood countertop.

Any species can make a decorative countertop, but tough woods make the best butcher-block countertops, with maple the standard (end-grain bamboo is very strong, too). Both end-grain and edge-grain butcher-block make excellent cutting surfaces, whereas face-grain wood works well as a serving or dining countertop. Work-surface wood countertops are typically unsealed but usually oiled with periodic rubdowns of mineral, tung, or linseed oil. Wood that won't be worked on directly can be sealed with polyurethane to protect it from moisture; be sure to finish all sides before installation to prevent warping. For an environmentally friendly wood, look for certification by the Forest Stewardship Council (FSC).

Wood backsplashes are most commonly vertical beadboard and occasionally horizontal wide boards. Satin or glossy paint and polyurethane make durable, easy-to-clean finishes for wood backsplashes.

Bamboo is technically a grass, but it's harder than most wood species and it matures much more quickly. Bamboo is ready to harvest in five years and regrows easily. A considerable amount of adhesive is required to laminate bamboo strands together, so look for low or no volatile organic compound (VOC) glues, if that's a concern. Bamboo can be laminated to show either end grain, edge grain, or flat grain. Treat a bamboo countertop like wood, with either an oil applied to a work surface or polyurethane applied to all sides.

An edge-grained maple butcher-block countertop maintains its good looks even around a sink due to regular oiling and diligent mopping up of spills. The restaurant-style faucet has an easy-to-direct spray.

ABOVE The different materials in these two countertop levels reflect use, with a solid-wood board at the dining level and soapstone at the work level and on the low backsplash. A vitreous china farmhouse sink is well served by a user-friendly single-lever faucet.

LEFT A stainless-steel wrapped board supports the edge-grained red oak butcher-block overhang on a big island, along with the help of handcrafted metal brackets.

ABOVE Stainless steel makes for a tough, easy-to-clean kitchen for hardworking cooks. Seamed panels are standard restaurant grade. Built-in rods keep kitchen tools at the ready. The stainless-steel countertop is edged with wood for a bit of warmth and softness.

FACING PAGE A trim urban townhouse shows its contemporary aesthetic with a square-edged stainless-steel countertop and stacked white subway tile backsplash. Modern faucet spouts are balanced by traditional separate hot and cold controls.

S tainless-steel countertops excel in home kitchens for the same reason they work in restaurant kitchens. Stainless steel stands up to heat and water like no other surface, yet it's cool enough for rolling out pie dough. It's durable and easy to keep scrupulously clean. Stainless steel can be formed with an integral sink or backsplash for ultimate watertightness. There's no way to avoid scratches, though, so go for a brushed surface, which disguises fingerprints and scratches much better than polished stainless.

A 16-gauge stainless-steel countertop will suit most kitchens. A stainless-steel countertop is formed around or supported by wood or MDF to add strength and mute sound. While stainless is unaffected by hot pans, be wary of putting very hot cast iron pans on zinc or copper because discoloration can occur. Factor length into the price, with 10 ft. being the cutoff before the price per square foot goes up. And edge profiles can have an impact on price and looks. Some homeowners love the modified marine edge, which is a rounded lip that keeps smaller spills on the countertop. Others prefer how the square or flat edged profile makes it easier to sweep kitchen trimmings into a pail or chopped food into a pot. A bullnose edge is best suited for countertops that won't see water, as that half-round profile can allow drips to make their way to cabinet faces.

Stainless steel is far and away the most popular of metal countertops, but other metals have their devotees. Copper is beautiful and warm and will develop a patina either naturally or purposefully with the application of chemicals or heat. Copper is soft, shows scratches, and is expensive. Zinc is softer than stainless steel and is more moderately priced. Zinc can't be scrubbed with abrasive cleaner, and seams can show due to zinc's variable color. Pewter is extremely expensive and easy to scratch, but it adds a European-kitchen look. Bronze oxidizes like copper but to a lesser degree; it's stronger than copper and somewhat more expensive.

A New England redo sacrificed one of its many windows to make room for a cheerful, decorative tile backsplash behind the gas cooktop. Countertops are black granite.

TILE

t ile is an age-old kitchen surface that never seems to lose its appeal, but these days it's seen much more on backsplashes than on countertops. The enormous variety of shapes, sizes, textures, and colors allows tile to fit any location and work with every kitchen style. Subway tile and glass tile retain their popularity in part because new sizes, shapes, and colors are created all the time, such as oversize subway tiles and super-thin, rectangular glass tiles.

Most tile is more economical than slab or engineered stone, solid surfacing, and stainless steel, and it's the perfect DIY material, although complex patterns can be tricky to do yourself. Glazed ceramic tiles and glass tiles are themselves nonporous (stone tile requires a sealer) but cement-based grout, the most commonly used type, needs to be sealed to resist staining and mildew, preferably with a penetrating sealer.

Epoxy grout and urethane grout don't require sealing and resist staining, but both of these grouts take expertise to use, so consider hiring a professional. Choosing grout color has a big impact on how tile is perceived. White and dark grouts can make a tiled backsplash look busier; if you're looking for a more subdued look, consider a gray-toned grout, even with white tile. Live with a sample board of grouted tile for a week or so before you make a commitment that will last a long time.

Keep cutting boards at hand when working on a tile countertop. It's a tough material but it can crack if something really heavy is dropped on it. Likewise, while tile is heat resistant, it's not heatproof, so it's a good idea to set out hot pads or trivets for when you take a cast-iron braising pot out of the oven.

RIGHT This mini butler's pantry is out in public, so it's finished handsomely with a glass-tile backsplash and granite countertop.

BELOW Glass tiles with a satin finish make a softly glowing backsplash in a coastal home. A narrow window allows a view but not the glaring Florida sun. The countertop is limestone.

ABOVE Varying thicknesses and colors of ceramic tile create a handsome and tough backsplash at the cooktop workstation. The countertop is Caesarstone® engineered quartz. Rather than interrupt tile work, electrical outlets are tucked under the wall cabinets.

A backsplash of custom handmade tile by a local artisan provides a backdrop for red ceramic lizard sculptures from Guatemala. Perimeter countertops are Absolute Black granite, while the island counter is a lighter, figured granite that matches the tone of the backsplash tile.

more about...
INSTALLING GLASS TILE

glass tile has been a hot backsplash material for almost a decade, and new colors and sizes continue to spark interest. Be aware that glass tile isn't quite the same species as ceramic tile, and that makes it less of a DIY-friendly material. Glass tiles are more reflective than ceramic tile and may reveal imperfections in the backboard, and glass reacts to temperature changes more dramatically than ceramic tile, so can't be squeezed too tightly together. Translucent glass tiles show what's behind, so use white thinset compound with any ridges smoothed out before tiles are set.

BELOW Cheerful green-and-yellow penny-round tiles cover this kitchen wall from the ceiling to the white engineered quartz countertops. Shelves with no visible supports were custom-built by the general contractor.

ABOVE A big, vitreous-china farmhouse sink is matched by a tall, restaurant-style faucet. The faucet is nickel plated for a traditional look, but its single-lever operation and tall sprayer are thoroughly modern. A water filter at left has hot and cold controls.

LEFT Colors in this Lagos Azul limestone backsplash vary slightly to create a subtle harmony. These mosaic stone tiles are tough but beautiful. The countertop is Danby marble, an especially dense marble.

more about...
PLASTIC LAMINATE

plastic laminate remains a popular countertop material largely because it's the most economical countertop choice. Plastic laminate is fairly easy to install, relatively stain-proof, easy to clean, and waterproof, unless a seam is compromised. On the downside, it's relatively soft, and scratches will show, so use cutting boards. Plastic laminate can't withstand super hot pots and pans. If you are concerned about chemical sensitivity, look for low-VOC glues and substrates.

Sure, plastic laminate isn't as glamorous as many countertop options, but it's worth a closer look at today's range of patterns, colors, finishes, and the wider variety of edge profiles. Choosing plastic laminate for work counters could make room in your budget for an expensive showpiece countertop on an island. Edges can be beveled or bullnose or edged with wood, metal, or another material. An upgrade option is heavy-duty plastic laminate, which is fabricated with a thicker, tougher top layer. And take a look at the growing availability of integral plastic-laminate sinks.

ABOVE White engineered quartz countertops and a wall filled with white, tan, and brown glass mosaic tiles create a bright, sophisticated urban kitchen. The undermount sink is a two-bowl stainless-steel model.

RIGHT Painted beadboard makes a traditional and sturdy backsplash, and finishing off the bottom with a tall, smooth-painted base makes it especially easy to clean up spills. The perimeter countertop is soapstone.

more about...
SOLID SURFACING

olid surfacing, made from polyester or acrylic resin plus a mineral filler and pigments, can be shaped to fit just about any layout and given almost any edge profile. Solid surfacing is completely nonporous, doesn't off-gas, and is easy to clean; small scratches can be sanded out. It's moderately resistant to heat (no just-out-of-the-oven pans, please). Because it's homogenous and fairly soft, solid surfacing is easy to repair and gentle on dishes. Larger abrasions or cracks will require professional repair. Solid surfacing is available in a wide variety of colors and finishes and a fairly wide range of prices. Although solid surfacing in years past would never pass for stone, today you can find patterns with plenty of movement that look more and more like stone, but there's no need for imitation, as solid surfacing is easy to appreciate for its solid, bright colors and agreeable softness. It's possible to fabricate solid surface countertops with integral sinks and backsplashes for waterproofing that rivals a stainless-steel countertop with integral sink.

A solid-surface countertop with an integral backsplash provides watertight joints. Dramatically figured marble makes a stand-out backsplash on the cooktop wall.

Edge-grain wood flanks the range, and the backsplash is tile. A beautifully cast 2-in.-thick concrete slab tops the island. Flooring is reclaimed antique heart pine. Over half the cabinetry is salvaged, in large part to avoid the off-gassing that new cabinetry can produce. Library sconces light glass-door wall cabinets.

more about...

CONCRETE

oncrete can make a breathtakingly beautiful countertop. It can take just about any color, texture, shape, and any number of objects can be cast into it from glass bits to shells. Concrete is also heat resistant and very durable, and as heavy as stone, so account for the extra weight when choosing cabinets. Its price varies, depending on what's in the concrete from aggregates to additives, and how much artistry and complexity are involved. Concrete stains, so it must be sealed carefully and periodically

with either a topical or penetrating sealer. Penetrating sealer allows for a much more natural look and is best accompanied by periodic waxing to bring out the beauty of concrete. Like wood, concrete will develop a patina over time. For either cast-in-place or precast concrete countertops, it's critical to find a reputable craftsperson, so call references and look at sample work.

ABOVE PaperStone composite countertops can be worked like wood, so they could be installed by a dedicated homeowner, although it certainly helps to be a woodworker, like the owner of this kitchen. After sealing, the countertops are resistant to water and staining.

PAPER, GLASS, AND METAL COMPOSITES

@ll kinds of materials are making their way into today's composite countertops, including recycled metals, recycled paper and cardboard, glass, and plant pulps, such as wheat paste and sorghum. Some composite countertop fabricators feature no urea-formaldehyde. Here are some popular composites.

Paper-based composite countertops are made with recycled paper, newspaper, or cardboard or with virgin paper, which makes a more uniform countertop. Paper-based countertops require finishing, which can vary among manufacturers. These countertops won't off-gas and are strong, food safe, and moderately heat resistant. Scratches can be repaired by sanding, then reapplying the finish. In fact, paper composite countertops can be installed by intrepid homeowners.

Recycled glass countertops are fabricated from recycled glass (sometimes mixed with virgin broken glass) mixed with cement binder or epoxy resin. Countertops made with cement binder are more durable but require sealing. Resin-bound counters don't require sealing, just periodic waxing for shine, but they aren't quite as tough, so don't cut on them.

Scrap metal countertops are typically made with aluminum shavings bound with resin. This thin material is installed on a plywood substrate. Scrap-metal composite counters don't require a sealer, but they can't be cut on and they aren't heatproof.

LEFT A straw-bale house in California features eco-friendly finishes, including no-VOC composite countertops of recycled paper. Countertop openings allow quick access to a compost container (right), garbage, and recycling containers. A short backsplash offers a narrow shelf against the wall and a visual shield at the peninsula.

more about...
ENGINEERED STONE OR QUARTZ COMPOSITE

e ngineered stone is technically a composite, but it's mostly stone, with 90% stone chips and ground stone powder. Most engineered stone is quartz based, so it's often called simply quartz or composite quartz. Engineered stone makes a countertop that is superior to slab stone in density and needs no sealing. It's extremely tough, hard to chip, and heat resistant. Engineered quartz is more consistent looking than stone, which can be a turnoff for some but a boon to others, who prefer a less busy countertop to balance more elaborate details, such as a bolder backsplash or cabinet door design. Engineered stone comes in colors and patterns that are stonelike but is also fabricated in bright, rich colors you won't find in any other countertop material. Surfaces can be polished, honed, or sandblasted.

Lime green engineered stone with a matching green mosaic-tile backsplash creates a cheerful prep and cooking space on an island. Polished granite on the higher surface and on the perimeter cabinets is a more traditional material, along with the glazed running-bond tile backsplash.

LEFT Engineered stone like this orange countertop has a unique brilliance that no natural material can match. This orange countertop is tough, waterproof, and stain-proof, and needs no sealing. The single-handle control is positioned in the front for ease of operation in a tight spot. A super-deep restaurant-quality sink features two different-size bowls.

BELOW Tiny stainless-steel tiles set in a running bond pattern create a sparkling but highly utilitarian backsplash in an urban kitchen. Receptacles on the sidewall and under cabinets keep the backsplash pristine. Countertops are engineered stone.

What makes stone so attractive is its individual character, so the key to being happy with your stone countertop or backsplash is to visit stoneyards to see stones up close, then to choose the exact slabs for your kitchen. Review drawings by your designer and stone installer to understand where seams will go and ask how the slabs will be seamed. Vein-matched seams are made from two sequential slabs polished on the same face, while bookmarked seams are made from two sequential slabs polished on opposite faces so that they mirror each other when seamed. If you plan on matching backsplash to countertop, consider the design possibilities as you study stone slabs.

If slab stone is just too expensive, consider stone tiles for your countertop or backsplash. Another economical stone option is prefab granite, which is cut and finished overseas, primarily in China. Like stock cabinets, prefab granite is available only in standard sizes but in a variety of finishes and several edge profiles. Prefab granite is thin and must be installed on ¾-in. plywood for strength, and it's usually doubled at the edge to resemble a thicker slab.

GRANITE

Granite has been king of countertop stones for a long time in pricier kitchens but now it's even landing on countertops in mid-range kitchens. Granite is a hugely variable stone in looks and temperament. It's quarried in many countries in many colors, patterns, and prices. Granite can be green friendly, or not. For example, a stone quarried in South America might travel the ocean to be finished on another continent before it makes its way to the United States. On the other hand, some granites may be available in your state. Granite is extremely hard and durable; it's a very tough stone to scratch. It's cool to the touch and can withstand heat well; on the downside, it's hard on dishware and can stain—oil is the biggest culprit—unless sealed well initially and regularly; how often depends on the type of granite.

MARBLE AND LIMESTONE

Marble and limestone have long been beautiful backsplash favorites, but as countertops they need special attention. Still, marble has been seeing more use on countertops because of its seductive good looks and cool temperature, ideal for rolling pastry dough. Just be aware that while marble isn't likely to stain if properly and regularly sealed, acidic foods will etch it, often even if you wipe up spills immediately. Just consider etching and small scratches as part of the patina that marble develops in a beautiful, well-used kitchen. A honed surface won't show etching and scratches as much as a polished surface. A rounded edge profile will not chip as easily as a square edge; this is especially important at an undermount sink, where pots and pans can do damage. Limestone is softer and more susceptible to etching than marble, but it too makes a beautiful backsplash or showcase countertop far from heavy-duty cooking.

SLATE AND SOAPSTONE

Slate and soapstone come in smaller slabs than granite, and in much more limited color ranges, but both can make beautiful, silky smooth, and durable countertops that require less care than many types of granite. Slate varies in density, and not all slates are suitable for countertops. But both countertop-worthy slate and soapstone are denser and hence less porous than granite and do not require sealing (certain slates may require sealing; seek out reliable sources). Slate and soapstone are softer to the touch than granite, too, which makes them a bit easier on dishware. Slate color depends on where it is quarried, with colors ranging from black to green to red. A traditional New England countertop for centuries, soapstone is light in tone when quarried and polished, but it oxidizes over time and turns dark, and veining will become more prominent. You'll want to hasten the darkening process by rubbing soapstone with mineral oil, boiled linseed oil, or a food-safe beeswax, with more applications early on and fewer as time goes by. As soapstone darkens, scratches are less apparent.

ABOVE Groove-textured black granite from Vermont makes a surface that's practically indestructible, smudge-proof, and easy to clean, and an impregnating sealer makes it impervious to water and acids.

ABOVE A polished granite countertop dresses up a small kitchen in a combined living/kitchen space. The undermount sink is deep enough to hide pots and pans from view during dinner.

RIGHT Stone tile makes a strong, handsome, and relatively economical countertop, as seen in this New England kitchen. Slate tile is trimmed by wood and the slate-tile backsplash is topped with a wood sill.

sinks

• • • A SINK IS THE MOST USED OF ALL kitchen tools, so it's important to make it work for you. First, consider adding a prep or bar sink, if there's room in both kitchen and budget. A prep sink should be close to both the cooktop and the main work surface, or it can be the centerpiece of a second prep area for a second cook. Trash/compost is best close to food prep. If your two sinks are far apart, locate the trash between the two sinks or consider two trash centers. Once you've nailed down how many sinks you want, determine their configuration and how they fit into the countertop and select the material that works for you and your countertop. And always shop for faucets at the same time you shop for sinks. All of these choices may be driven by location, as you'll want to consider countertop material and depth as you select sinks and faucets. Locate the main sink where you don't mind the view. In front of a window is traditional for a wash-up sink, but overlooking the rest of the kitchen or family room may work better for you. Provide 2 ft. on both sides of a wash-up sink for dishes, whether dirty or drying.

An oversize stainless-steel farmhouse sink is surrounded by a Carrara marble countertop with a hefty doubled edge.

ABOVE In a Minneapolis butler's pantry, an undermount bar sink is fit up with a gooseneck faucet with single side handle and a hot/cold purified water dispenser. Glazed gray subway tiles are set in a running bond pattern. Undercabinet lighting and receptacles add wall-to-wall convenience. The countertop is honed black granite.

ABOVE A carved travertine sink makes for an elegant centerpiece in a large country kitchen. Window hardware prevents locating a faucet at the back of the sink, so a side-mounted faucet with a long neck and a separate sprayer provide plenty of reach.

•sink materials

Stainless steel makes the ideal sink, according to most homeowners. It's non-porous, easy to clean, tough but easy on dropped dishes, immune to heat, and comes in a wide range of sizes, configurations, and prices. A 6-in.-deep, rectangular, single-bowl, 18-gauge model is a popular choice, durable, tough enough, and big enough for pots and pans. A 16-gauge sink (the lower the gauge number, the thicker the steel) is a sturdier model. A single wide bowl is more versatile that a multi-bowl model, and you can always fit it up with accessories that divide the space. A sink with sharp inside corners may look stylish, but it will be harder to clean; choose a small radius as a compromise. It's hard to imagine not finding the ideal configuration for your kitchen among manufactured sinks, but you can hire a local shop to custom fabricate a sink. Go for a number 4 brushed surface, as polished stainless steel in a sink will never look immaculate.

Copper, nickel, and bronze sinks can be stunning, but the cost is high, sometimes breathtakingly high, and upkeep is far more demanding than for stainless steel. Copper will oxidize to a dramatic degree, requiring either regular polishing or offering the beauty of a changing patina.

Like an integral stainless-steel sink and countertop, a **solid-surface** sink that's integral with a solid-surface counter creates a waterproof, easy-to-clean combo. Solid-surface sinks are not cheap, but they are easy on dropped dishes, and they're nonporous and stain resistant and small scratches won't show up because the material is homogenous. Modest scratches can be sanded out while a licensed fabricator can repair more serious damage.

Acrylic sinks are inexpensive, nonporous, and available in a number of configurations, but they are also soft and vulnerable to abrasive cleaners and petroleum-based products. In addition, they can't withstand pots straight from the cooktop. Look for the more expensive acrylic sinks that claim to resist staining and scratching.

Enameled sinks are a breeze to clean and to keep looking clean. They're very difficult to scratch. It's tough to damage them, but enameled sinks can chip and potentially expose the metal to rust. Enameled cast-iron is merciless on dropped glasses, but you can avoid that with a springy metal rack in the sink bottom. Enameled steel sinks are much lighter than cast iron and usually less expensive, but can be noisy unless a sound-deadening material is applied to the underside.

Stone can be carved into a sink (for a mind-boggling price tag), but a stone sink is more likely fabricated from flat slabs into an apron-front configuration. Soapstone is a traditional sink material that's easy to work yet extremely dense, and it's comparatively gentle on dropped dishes. Any stone sink requires extra support and that structure may reduce cabinet space below.

Engineered stone sinks are a mix of a high proportion of powdered stone (usually quartz or granite) with a small amount of resin. These sinks are tough, strong, don't need sealing, and won't stain.

Ceramic sinks are lovely and can be cast with intricate details. Ceramic sinks are heavy, tough on dropped dishes, and susceptible to cracks if hot water is poured in a cold sink or a hot pan is set down in it. A metal grid that fits into the bottom of the sink can prevent dings, broken dishware, and thwart heat-related cracking. Some ceramic sink owners report that the vibration of a garbage disposal can cause cracking.

LEFT A run-down Cape Cod house was renovated with traditional New England details, including an authentically traditional countertop, backsplash, and sink, with a wall-mounted two-handled faucet.

FACING PAGE An 800-sq.-ft. cottage for a downsizing retired couple required serious cooking tools, so while the floor area is minimal, the sink is a generous vitreous-china farmhouse model, with an elegant bridge faucet to match. The countertops are slate, and the backsplash is ceramic tile.

ABOVE A new farmhouse-style vitreous-china sink is cast with a reproduction-worthy backsplash designed for a modern faucet set.

• sink configurations

A 33-in.-wide, 10-in.-deep single-bowl sink is the most versatile of sinks. There's room for soaking large cookie sheets, grill racks, and big stock pots, and there's space to hide dinner party dishes until it's time to wash up. Sinks with wide-radiused inside corners may look capacious but may not fit a large pan. Take your favorite large roasting pan to the showroom to check it out or take measurements of your favorite baking gear. But if every pot and pan goes straight into the dishwasher, you may be happy with a two-bowl sink. A sink wider than 33 in. will require a wider-than-standard sink base cabinet. Consider where the drain is located. Most sinks have centered drains but a drain off to the side makes it easier to soak a pan For sink installation options, see the drawing on the facing page.

ABOVE This round, second sink is ideal for food prep near the cooktop. A wall-mounted faucet keeps the countertop clear.

SINK INSTALLATION TYPES

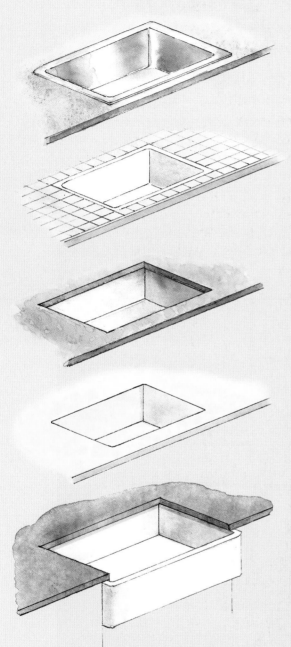

DROP-IN OR SELF-RIMMING SINK

Countertop materials that have a vulnerable edge, such as plastic-laminate and wood, require a self-rimming sink (exception: integrated plastic-laminate sinks are available in limited styles). Steel sinks can be clipped into place and trimmed with a separate piece or are self-rimming, a neater but more expensive option. Porcelain-enamel cast-iron sinks remain in place by their weight. The lip around a self-rimming sink can be hard to keep clean. All drop-in and self-mounting sinks should be sealed under the lip with silicone caulk.

FLUSH-MOUNT SINK

Flush-mount sinks, also called tile-edge or tiled-in sinks, are designed to drop in onto the substrate and to be flush with a tile countertop. Tile is installed flush with the sink, which may require shimming to align properly with the tile. Caulk between the tile and the sink edge makes the joint waterproof.

UNDERMOUNT SINK

Undermount sinks make it easy to clean off the countertop but may require extra attention to keep the obscured top edge of the sink clean. The tricky part of this sink option is cutting the hole for the sink properly, either off-site or in place. Countertop materials that require sealing on the surface must be sealed at the cut edge. Heavy sinks require support from below. Because the sink is set lower than a drop-in sink, its greater depth will require you to bend over more.

INTEGRAL SINK

Stainless-steel or other metals can be shopmade or manufactured into many configurations of integral sink, backsplash, and countertop. Solid-surface, composite stone, and some plastic laminate countertops can be shop fabricated with integral sinks. These sinks have either no joints or extremely tightly glued joints so they don't leak and don't have joints to clean around.

FARMHOUSE OR APRON-FRONT SINK

The farmhouse, or apron-front, sink protrudes from the countertop and cabinetry, so its material and finish are important design features. These sinks make it easier to get close to produce or dishes for washing but can wet your shirt when you belly up to the sink, and they tend to be more costly, both for the fixture and for the specialized base cabinet below.

Groove-textured Vermont black granite provides a visual ballast to light-toned anigre-veneer cabinets and a glass backsplash, which is finished on the back with a white coating. The single-lever faucet has a pull-out sprayer.

RIGHT A generous single-handled faucet with pull-out sprayer provides plenty of reach—enough, in fact, to fill a vase or pot on the countertop. The countertop is Danby marble and the backsplash is Lagos Azul limestone mosaic tile.

FACING PAGE Once a dining space, this new kitchen in a Tudor revival home is big enough for serious cooking. The island table is topped with recycled barn boards and the countertop and sink are fabricated from Woodland Jade slate. The generously proportioned single-handled faucet has a pull-down sprayer. Cabinets are quartersawn white oak with a dark glaze.

FAUCET AND SPRAYER CHOICES

the traditional faucet is operated by two handles, but a single handle or lever is today's runaway favorite. Even easier to turn on is a hands-free faucet.

SINGLE LEVER, SINGLE HANDLE

Single-lever faucets have a lower arc than a gooseneck faucet, and the lever is positioned behind and above the spout. These are easier to reach than side-mounted handles, which are the norm for a gooseneck, high-arch spout. But gooseneck spouts are popular for their looks and the ability to set a tall pot in the sink for washing (most sprayers make it easy to fill a tall pot on the countertop). Some homeowners prefer to move the side-mounted handle to the front to make it easier to operate and to avoid water dripping on the countertop from wet hands.

THE HANDS-FREE FAUCET

A big help to a serious cook, a hands-free faucet is either operated by a motion sensor or by a foot pedal or lever. Either device can be turned off if your guests have a hard time operating it, and a foot pedal can be locked on for a continuous stream without your having to keep your foot in position, then unlocked, so that you can instantly control the water with your foot again. Aside from thwarting the spread of bacteria, a hands-free faucet means there are fewer fingerprints and water spots to clean off the spout and handle.

SPRAYERS

Sprayers can be separately installed on the countertop or sink rim, but the hottest kitchen wish-list item is a pull-down sprayer (or a pull-out for a less arched faucet). The head of the faucet pulls down to become a sprayer attached to a flexible hose; a braided stainless-steel hose is very durable—and pricey. The pull-down sprayer extends the reach of the faucet by a significant amount, making it possible to fill a tall pot sitting on the countertop. Most faucet sprayers can change from stream to spray with the touch of a button.

cooking appliances

● ● ● THE FIRST CHOICE TO MAKE WHEN choosing cooking appliances is between a range or separate cooktop and wall oven. Whether it's a luxurious centerpiece with multiple burners and fuel sources or a basic economical and space-saving model, what makes a range appealing is that it focuses cooking and heat in one spot. But a two-cook kitchen may be better served by separate units: a cooktop, one or more wall ovens, and perhaps a specialized oven. Separate cooking appliances will require additional installation, but they also offer more flexibility of source, fuel, size, and location. Wall ovens can fit into a bank of wall cabinets or tuck under a countertop. Smaller accessory ovens, including microwave, steam, speed, and warming ovens can fit into cabinetry above a wall oven but they often function more comfortably when placed just under the countertop. Whatever cooking appliances you choose, be sure to buy a fire extinguisher, and store it near an exit, not adjacent to cooking equipment.

ABOVE The homeowner-architect designed and built this range hood at a considerable savings. Tempered glass makes an economical and easy-to-clean backsplash.

RIGHT A suspended hood is powerful enough to properly ventilate an island cooktop in a small kitchen. To the right is a pot rack.

FACING PAGE These appliances are Energy Star® rated. The microwave is a freestanding model, as is the refrigerator. Near the range (at left), a lowered secondary prep countertop is open below to make room for a wheelchair.

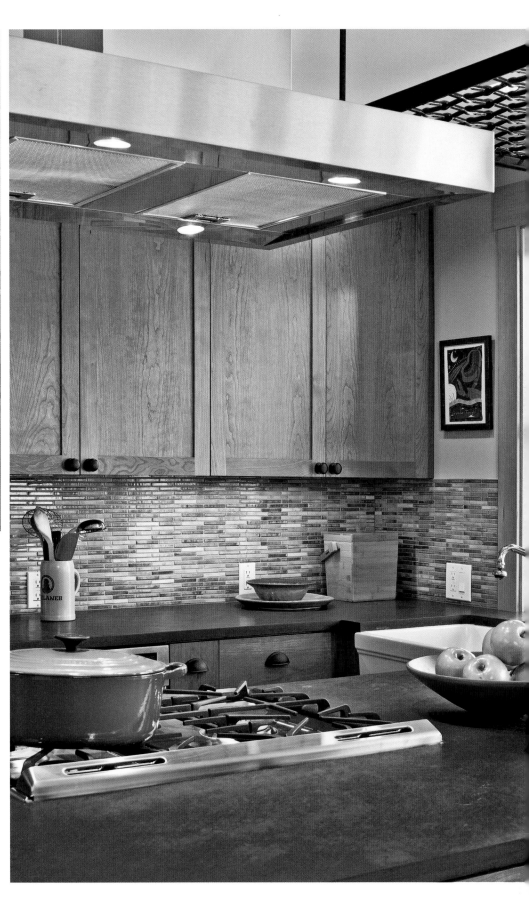

Microwave cooking and range cooking don't cross paths in this cheery family kitchen. The range is on an outside wall for direct ventilation, and an abundance of windows affords the cook a serene view. The microwave oven is a freestanding model tucked into a finished niche.

ABOVE Two wall ovens and a cooktop take the place of a range in this California kitchen. A built-in hood is well concealed by woodwork.

LEFT Two wall ovens and a warming drawer make a tidy stack next to the pantry and across from the range. A small island at right and a countertop to the right of the cooktop provide landing space.

• ranges

There's no need to purchase a separate cooktop and wall oven simply because you prefer a gas cooktop for speedy response and an electric oven for steady temperature. Today's ranges offer dual fuel sources, even on the cooktop itself. And range configurations have changed to suit the times, with some moderately priced ranges boasting a warming drawer or two stacked ovens.

Keep in mind that some ranges are taller and deeper than the typical base cabinet with countertop, and a freestanding range may not fit tidily into a spot once held by a slide-in range. Compare existing conditions to exact product specs, and ask about filler pieces and retrofit options. It's easier to accommodate bigger ranges in new cabinetry, as base cabinets can be installed proud of the wall an inch or two (or on higher toe space bases). Of course, this requires a deeper countertop.

True commercial ranges belong in commercial kitchens, not homes, as they aren't insulated and can be extremely hot to the touch, even to the point of scorching adjacent cabinets. Professional-style ranges are insulated and have pilotless ignitions, and consumer-friendly features such as oven windows, oven lights, and broilers.

LEFT A blue French range makes a fashion statement but it's also a tool for a serious cook. An updraft vent and a range hood vent handle heavy-duty cooking tasks.

ABOVE Any cooktop requires a serviceable backsplash that's waterproof and stain resistant like this European tile behind a Lacanche range. A pot filler makes it easy to fill large vessels.

FACING PAGE While the four-burner gas/ electric range is industrial stainless steel, the range hood is finished with white paneling and trim to maintain the kitchen's traditional Scandinavian-influenced style.

• cooktops

Cooktop configurations vary widely depending on overall width and fuel source. Look for a cooktop that has at least two high-powered burners and one that can simmer steadily, or even just provide enough heat to keep a pan warm. Some models offer two large burners in front, but most offer one large burner and one smaller burner in front and the same configuration in reverse in back. Standard electric cooktops may offer bridge elements, which tie together two burners to make a burner big enough for making gravy in a roasting pan. A gas cooktop may feature a continuous grate that makes it easy to handle that wide roasting pan, or to push a big pot off the burner. Note that controls on the front or side are much easier to access for anyone with limited movement.

Cooktops can be installed into a countertop like a drop-in sink, with the countertop surrounding all sides, or like an apron-front sink, with the countertop interrupted by the unit. Apron-front cooktops require closer coordination between countertop depth and cabinet construction. Take care that any back-splash behind a cooktop is resistant to heat, moisture, and stains. Allow for a landing space that's at least 9 in. on one side and 15 in. on the other, with 9 in. behind the cooktop if it's on an island or peninsula. But go beyond the minimums if you can, with 18 in. on each side. If there's bar seating behind the cooktop, provide at least 24 in. of space.

Cooktops can be fueled by gas (natural or propane) or powered by electricity. Electric cooktops can be inexpensive electric coil, standard electric smooth top, or induction, the electromagnetic-powered kid on the cooktop block. The cost of power and availability of gas in your neighborhood may factor in to which cooktop you choose.

This cooktop can be set entirely within the countertop for a less obtrusive presence with room below for a cooking utensil drawer.

RIGHT In a tiny urban kitchen, the window acts as both backsplash and ventilation for a five-burner cooktop. Glass tile at the left resists heat, stains, and water.

BELOW The homeowner-architect of this kitchen found these high-quality appliances at a discount online and in appliance stores. He positioned the gas cooktop above the separate wall oven as if it were a range.

more about...
GAS COOKTOPS

ntil the induction cooktop came along, the gas cooktop was far superior to the electric cooktop for instant and infinite control. Gas still has advantages over induction cooking. Gas is usually available during a power outage, cooktops can be significantly less expensive than induction models, and gas doesn't require iron-based cookware. And some cooks still prefer the direct view and control of a cooking flame. Gas cooktops also offer a variety of specialized accessories, such as a grill, griddle, deep fryer, steamer, or wok. A gas cooktop can include an induction element or two, so you can have the best of both worlds.

more about...
ELECTRIC
COOKTOPS

S tandard electric coil and smooth-top cooktops are
quick to heat but slow to respond. However, they don't
off-gas, which could be of benefit to asthma sufferers. Smooth
tops are easier to clean than coils, especially if spills are
attended to quickly; dark and speckled surfaces hide scratches
and dirt better than white smooth tops; the ceramic glass
smooth top requires more care in handling heavy or scratchy
pots than do coil and gas cooktops.

**This cooktop is in a niche that's
perfect for efficient ventilation, a
real necessity in an urban kitchen.
From across the room, the hood
vent is completely invisible.**

An induction cooktop is super fast to heat, yet it remains cool to the touch because it heats only the contents inside the cooking vessel; the pot must contain a high iron content.

INDUCTION COOKTOPS

nduction cooktops are powered by electromagnetic energy, which causes ferrous (iron-based) cookware to heat up. Induction is much more energy efficient—almost twice—than gas or traditional electric cooktops. This means that a large pot of water can come to a boil in a couple of minutes, whereas a gas or standard electric cooktop will take at least twice as long. The burners are topped by a ceramic glass surface like a smooth-top electric. Not only do induction cooktops heat rapidly but they provide consistent heat, are quick to respond, don't heat the air, and offer easy cleanup because spilled food won't burn and stick to the cooktop, which is cool to the touch. Because the electromagnetic energy heats cookware, the surface of the cooktop is not super hot, although there will be residual heat from the hot pot itself. This makes an induction

cooktop a good choice if you are concerned about universal design standards. Look for a model with finely tuned power gradations and a timer that turns off burners.

Induction could be the ideal cooking method, but it remains much more expensive than gas and standard electric cooktops. While induction costs less to run, it would take years to recoup the difference. Induction cooktops also require flat-bottomed ferrous cookware, so take a magnet shopping. High settings and lighter-weight cookware have been associated with an audible buzz, so check out an operating induction cooktop before you buy. If you aren't sure about induction or would like to mix induction with more conventional cooktop burners, look for cooktops that combine gas or standard burners with one or two induction burners.

• ovens

Once or twice a year, a standard radiant oven big enough for a turkey and side dishes comes in mighty handy. But more often, you'll wish for two ovens for cooking different foods at different temperatures. A smaller oven is more energy efficient and retains moisture better, too. Wall ovens are available at all price points, and some 30-in. and 36-in. ranges offer two ovens, usually stacked. Larger pro-style ranges and heavy-duty European models have several small ovens both stacked and side by side.

The standard oven is a radiant, or thermal oven, which cooks by a combination of radiant energy from a heat source—an electric element at the bottom and top (for broiling) or gas-fired flame under the oven floor. Convection ovens incorporate a fan in an electric radiant oven; a true convection oven has a third heating element that heats air before it circulates. Naturally, the true convection is more efficient.

This gas cooktop is paired with a wall oven for a range-like cooking setup, but there's an additional wall oven and a speed/microwave oven close by, set in base cabinets to keep the walls clear for flip-door frosted-glass cabinets.

m o r e   a b o u t ...

MICROWAVE OVENS

@ microwave oven is a given in most kitchens. Sometimes it's even the prime oven, especially as new technologies are marrying fast-cooking microwaves with other technologies such as convection and steam heat, which boost the taste and visual appeal beyond standard microwave fare. The big question is where to put the microwave, conventional or not? An over-the-range (OTR) microwave oven makes sense in a small kitchen, but in a larger kitchen, consider a location that's easier to reach and out of the path of the primary cook. Built-in microwaves tend to be deeper than wall cabinets, so will fit more neatly in

base cabinets, island cabinetry, or in a deep wall of cabinets that likely includes a wall oven or two. Microwave drawers fit into base cabinets, ideally at the end of a run of cabinets or in an island, away from the main cooking path but with a landing space immediately above.

Instead of going for a built-in microwave oven, consider tucking a freestanding model into a finished custom-built niche in the base cabinet. Provide an outlet at the back of the niche, plus room for the cord, and a freestanding microwave oven will look much like a built-in, but it'll be easier to replace when its time is up.

ABOVE The most favored appliance in the morning, this coffee center is built into a wall of overlay frameless pantry cabinets.

WARMING DRAWERS AND SPECIALTY OVENS

@ warming oven, also called a warming drawer, has various settings from moist to crisp and can keep food at a safe temperature while the rest of dinner is prepared or until diners arrive. If keeping foods crisp is an option you'd like, look for a model with a vent for releasing steam. Warming drawers are also handy for warming plates and coffee cups, proofing bread dough, defrosting food gently, and drying bread crumbs. A range with a built-in warming drawer can be an economical option, but a separate warming drawer has the benefit of being positioned at a more comfortable level, such as just under the countertop.

Hot new oven technologies will be tempting to the busy and adventurous cook. Most intriguing to avid cooks in a hurry are speed ovens and steam ovens. Steam ovens incorporate steam from a reservoir or plumbed water line (the latter is more expensive). The more flexible hybrid steam-convection oven provides two technologies: a roast chicken can be first steamed for juicy tenderness, then browned crisp by convection. Either function can be used alone, and manufacturers tout them for all foods, including sweets, breads, rice, meats, and vegetables. Speed ovens can incorporate microwave energy, steam, convection, and high-intensity radiant heat, such as halogen bulbs. A built-in coffee center focuses on a narrow cooking task, but it could be just the thing to ease a busy morning schedule. Many systems require no water supply so can be located anywhere; plumbed water supply is more convenient but more costly. Some units offer a place to warm a cup and plate.

LEFT This freestanding microwave oven rests on a shelf in a stock IKEA cabinet case. Blocking keeps the microwave away from the walls to allow for ventilation.

refrigerators and freezers

●●● THE REFRIGERATOR HAS SEEN MANY changes in size and looks over time, but the two biggest changes are in configuration and efficiency. Refrigerator and freezer interiors are finely tuned today, with drawers, moveable shelves, variable temperatures and humidity levels, and electronic controls. Stainless steel adds to the price of a refrigerator, and takes more time to keep clean than white and black finishes, but it adds a professional gleam to a kitchen. Brushed stainless doesn't show fingerprints like polished stainless steel, making it a better choice for your refrigerator.

External refrigerator configurations have undergone transformations, too, with refrigerator and freezer drawers being the most radical and popular new ways to keep food cold. For entertaining, look to the many widths and heights of wine coolers and to trash compactor–size ice makers.

ABOVE This refrigerator/freezer is built in. While it's covered with panels that match surrounding cabinetry, it's still possible to tell it's a fridge and not a pantry.

ABOVE This tiny urban kitchen is well served by two undercabinet-size fridge and freezer compartments. The island serves as landing space for several appliances.

FACING PAGE This freestanding, standard-depth 27-in. refrigerator stands proud of the 24-in. cabinetry in its full stainless-steel glory. The French-door model is an especially handy design for a small kitchen.

RIGHT This professional-style built-in refrigerator/ freezer unit also incorporates a wine cooler. There's a landing space to the left of the fridge or on the island opposite.

BELOW Matching mahogany panels keep this built-in refrigerator/freezer in harmony with the rest of the cabinetry.

h ow the refrigerator fits into cabinetry is a question of aesthetics and budget. The standard fridge is 27 in. deep, deeper than the standard 24-in.-deep cabinet. A pricier alternative is a freestanding cabinet-depth (about 24 in.) refrigerator. Costlier still is the built-in fridge, with or without panels that match cabinets. Another notch up in cost is the trendy integrated refrigerator, which is completely covered by cabinetry, with no edges or seams visible. Cabinet-depth fridges make it easier to locate and retrieve food because food can't hide in the back. But cabinet-depth units may not easily fit a baking sheet or party tray. All the more reason to measure your platters and take those measurements to the appliance showroom because it's tough to really tell refrigerator configurations online or in a catalog. Another way around this is to set standard cabinets a few inches away from the wall to align with a standard-depth fridge. Be sure to provide landing space on the opening side of the fridge—at least 15 in.—or on a countertop across from the fridge but no farther than 4 ft. away.

RIGHT Undercabinet refrigerator drawers can be a placed away from the major food-prep area to reduce traffic jams. If they are fully integrated, only the family knows where they are.

FACING PAGE This standard-depth freestanding refrigerator/freezer fits neatly into cabinetry that was constructed deeper to match, giving it a more built-in look.

FOR REFRIGERATORS

refrigerators are much more energy efficient than their ancestors from two decades ago, and they keep getting more efficient, thanks to stronger energy standards. For each refrigerator on your shortlist, compare the energy statistics found on the EnergyGuide, a yellow tag that's available in showrooms and in product literature in print and online. Note that Energy Star ratings compare refrigerators with other refrigerators in the same category, and some refrigerator configurations are considerable more energy efficient than others.

Top-freezer refrigerators are the most energy efficient models, whereas side-by-side refrigerators are the least efficient. In-door ice and water dispensers add 15% or more to the energy bill and are the parts most often in need of

repairs. The easier it is to retrieve food, the less time the door stays open, so consider models with pull-out and elevator shelves, see-through drawers and good lighting. For bottom freezers, look for a two-drawer model so frozen items don't get deeply buried. Keep refrigerators away from heat-generating appliances and out of sunlight. Make sure there's enough air space around all appliances to vent ambient heat. Of course, the biggest contributor to energy use is size, so think smaller if it suits you. A smaller fridge may require more frequent shopping, probably by car, so it may not be more efficient within the larger energy equation. You'll have to do the math. Refrigerator electronics are controlled by computer chips that can be disturbed by power outages, so consider a surge-protected receptacle or even a whole-house surge suppressor.

FACING PAGE Here's a standard-depth freestanding refrigerator that's paired with cabinetry designed to be deeper than 2 ft. A freezer-over-fridge design is the most energy efficient.

RIGHT The only feature that gives away the presence of this integrated refrigerator/two-drawer freezer is the ventilation grille at the base. The cabinet at the top is just for storage.

BELOW A big side-by-side refrigerator is positioned at the end of a run of cabinets to make it easy to reach by cooks and noncooks alike.

more about...
WINE COOLERS

t he standard undercounter built-in wine cooler (also called a wine chiller or a wine refrigerator) is the size of a dishwasher, and most hold 28 to 60 bottles, depending on the bottle size. Most built-in models are stainless steel with glass-paneled doors, but some models can be paneled with a door that matches the cabinetry. Note that while a built-in wine cooler vents out the front, freestanding models usually vent out the rear and should not be completely built into cabinetry. You might want to locate a wine cooler close to dining, but be aware that a wine cooler makes some noise, like any refrigerator.

dishwashers

●●● LOCATING A DISHWASHER SHOULDN'T take too much mulling over, should it? Right next to the sink is the logical place. But which side of the sink? And if you're contemplating buying dishwasher drawers, consider placing one on each side of the sink. This arrangement is a universal design suggestion, as it doesn't require bending over as far to load and unload dishes. Another universal design suggestion for ease of use is to install the dishwasher 6 in. to 10 in. above the floor level. Of course, two full-size dishwashers might suit a prolific cook. Just fill one dishwasher with dirty dishes, wash, then use those clean dishes, meanwhile fill the second dishwasher. (The trick is to remember which is which.) Separating dishwashers will cost more due to additional plumbing and electrical work.

If possible, arrange dish storage within easy reach of the dishwasher, making it a one-step process to empty the dishwasher. The standard dishwasher is 24 in. wide but slimmer 18-in. models are available for tight spaces, and extra-wide dishwashers are available too. Haul much-used platters and dishes to a showroom to test the variety of rack configurations found in different dishwasher models. Some dishwashers have racks that can move down to make room for plates on the top, and others have tines that fold out of the way to make room for pots and pans, and many have shallow third racks for cutlery, which cuts down on the tendency of cutlery to spoon and prevent thorough washing. Some manufacturers offer a steam option, which is a gentle way to wash fragile stemware.

Raising dishwasher drawers well above the floor makes cleaning up and unloading much easier on the back. The raised countertop is handy for taller cooks.

ABOVE This farmhouse sink-dishwasher setup is situated for convenience, with dish storage in close-by wall cabinets and a big serving countertop a pivot away.

LEFT The big stainless-steel range makes a design statement in this cozy farmhouse kitchen, but the dishwasher maintains a low-key role, finished with panels that match the cabinetry.

green ideas...
FOR DISHWASHERS

ederal standards have resulted in a decade of improving energy efficiency in dishwashers, to such a degree that this year's models use 35% to 45% less water and energy than a dishwasher 10 years old. Study the yellow EnergyGuide label for comparative energy use. Energy Star dishwashers use about two-thirds of the water of dishwashers that didn't make the cut. Many of today's dishwashers have sensors that analyze the water at certain points in the cycle to tailor the amount of water and detergent. Newer dishwashers tend to have longer cycles that actually improve cleaning ability and use less water and energy.

Save water and energy by letting the dishwasher do its stuff. A dishwasher uses less water—and less heat—than handwashing, so just scrape food off plates and stick them in the dishwasher, unrinsed. Wash full loads; if the dishwasher isn't full, use the prerinse feature overnight; it uses less water than handwashing. Air drying dishes uses less energy than heat drying.

floors, walls, and ceilings

• • •

A KITCHEN FLOOR'S PRIMARY JOB IS TO BE SERVICEABLE. A FLOOR should resist stains and water, support your aching feet and back, withstand the dings of dropped kitchenware, and stand up to heavy traffic from humans and dogs. That's already a lot to ask, but you'll also want your kitchen floor to look good, especially if it's part of a larger living space. Wall coverings and ceiling finishes are often chosen last, but why wait? Considering how much square footage they cover, these surfaces deserve your careful consideration of materials, finishes, and colors. There's no need to stick to just one finish, of course. Wainscoting topped by a chair rail or picture rail makes a durable, handsome, and traditional finish in a dining-nook. Apply paint above the wainscoting where spills and dings aren't likely to occur. But paint itself can be a fine wall covering in a kitchen. In fact, if there's a finish or material you just can't pin down—it's likely to be a backsplash—don't leave the drywall patched and bare. Instead, give that strip of wall a prime coat and one or two coats of easy-to-clean satin or semigloss paint, perhaps in a color that matches one of the tiles you're considering for the area. You may decide that paint is just the thing for your kitchen's style and for your budget. Although a ceiling is likely to be simply painted, consider beadboard as a finish, or shape the space with a coffered or paneled ceiling.

Because walls and floors cover so much square footage, their color and texture have a big impact. This polished maple flooring is warm and traditional, and the clear, bright wall colors were chosen to reflect the work of traditional Scandinavian artist Carl Larsson.

floors

••• ALTHOUGH FLOORING HAS A BIG IMPACT on a kitchen's looks, it can have an even bigger impact on how you feel at the end of the day. Is it easy to stand on for hours? Is it easy to sweep clean and wipe up spills? For durability and longevity, ceramic and stone tile last for eons, but neither is that comfortable to stand on for long stretches. If comfort is key, choose a softer floor material such as resilient flooring (cork, vinyl, linoleum, or rubber), laminated flooring, or wood flooring. Wood is again a popular kitchen flooring because it's warm and comfortable, but largely because it can make a kitchen fit visually with a living space. Whatever the material, keep in mind that a floor covers a lot of ground, so a few dollars' difference per square foot can add up.

Flooring usually goes in first and generally from wall to wall; in the case of high-cost flooring, cabinet and appliance footprints can be filled in flush with plywood, but that limits future renovation. It's critical that flooring be well protected during the rest of construction; don't remove protective covers until the chandelier is up and switch plates are installed. If cabinets go in first and flooring last, there's less of a chance that flooring will be damaged, but the downsides are that flooring installation is trickier and future replacement cabinets must be located in the exact footprint (cabinets again are installed on plywood bases that match flooring).

BELOW Wide-plank hickory flooring creates a warm, traditional, and elegant floor. Oyster white walls pick up the gray of the stainless steel in subtle contrast to the white woodwork.

RIGHT Board-and-batten paneling provides a surface that's more durable than drywall or plaster. The wide plank flooring and exposed-beam ceiling suit this traditional Vermont kitchen.

ABOVE This transitional-traditional kitchen features contrasts in tone but the colors are neutral. The floor is walnut, the backsplash is subway tile, and the ceiling is a combination of materials, with beadboard over the hallway and dove gray paint over the kitchen proper.

RIGHT An exposed-beam ceiling gives this kitchen an Old World charm to match the traditional cabinetry and diamond-tile backsplash. Ceiling downlights are white to make them less obvious.

WOOD FLOORING: SOLID AND ENGINEERED

Wood flooring is beloved for its warmth, resilience, and ability to be refinished again and again and because it can make a kitchen blend more seamlessly with the rest of the house. Wood flooring can be solid or engineered. Most solid wood flooring is oak strip (¾ in. thick and 2½ in. wide); wider planks are a more traditional, and more expensive, option. The hardwoods maple, cherry, and hickory are popular in kitchens, too. Softwoods like heart pine and fir are lovely and traditional, but they are softer and more susceptible to denting.

Engineered wood looks like solid wood but actually consists of a thin layer of solid appearance-grade wood laminated to several layers of plywood, making it more dimensionally stable than solid wood. It's tricky to refinish this flooring because the top layer is so thin.

Both solid and engineered wood flooring can be either prefinished or unfinished, although engineered wood flooring is almost always prefinished. Prefinished wood flooring is good to go as soon as it's installed, and its finish is super tough, but the joints can be vulnerable to water damage. Finishing wood flooring in place takes time, smells, and requires staying off the floor for a few days. Although this isn't quite as tough as a factory finish, it provides better overall protection because joints are sealed along with strips.

What keeps any kind of wood looking good is frequent vacuuming and damp mopping, quick attention to spills, avoiding outdoor shoes, and, ultimately, refinishing. Area rugs also help. As with any surface, glossy finishes and dark tones show scratches and stains more than medium tones and satin finishes.

more about...
BAMBOO AND PALM FLOORING

bamboo may be a grass, but it has much in common with wood and is even called "timber bamboo" when grown in sustainable plantations, mostly in China and South America. It's the fastest-growing plant on Earth so it might seem sustainable, but transportation costs reduce its green rating (look for U.S.-grown bamboo in the future). Hardness varies: Strand-woven bamboo and end-grain bamboo have superior density and durability, but flat-grain and vertical-grain bamboo are less expensive. Each type has a different visual appeal. Like wood flooring, bamboo can be floating, nailed, or glued, and it can be prefinished or finished in place. Newer on the kitchen flooring scene is palm flooring, the product of old palm trees past their coconut-producing years. Lumber from the felled trees is laminated like plywood and is similar to other wood species in its finishing and maintenance.

ABOVE Cork flooring is comfortable to stand on, warm to bare feet, and looks great, too. Here, it creates a rich contrast to the cool green and white of this modern kitchen.

LEFT This rubber floor is tough, slip resistant, and looks both industrial and fun. When the wood-veneered door is open, kitchen and dining share light and space. Closed even part way, the door's horizontal grain adds interest and screening.

ABOVE Linoleum makes a warm, soft, comfortable, hypoallergenic floor, and it's made of natural materials. This linoleum repeats the warm colors of the cabinets and glass tile.

RIGHT One of linoleum's best qualities is its ability to be colored any tint. This rich, pure azure livens up a serious kitchen of stainless steel, black, and white.

m o r e   a b o u t . . .
RESILIENT FLOORING:
CORK, RUBBER, VINYL, AND LINOLEUM

esilient flooring is a favorite in kitchens because it's comfortable to stand on, easy to install, and relatively inexpensive compared to other flooring materials. Resilient flooring can have a long life if maintained by regular sweeping and damp mopping to remove grit, and if spills are wiped up from seams quickly. Most resilient flooring is available as tiles or sheets, and some are available as floating-floor planks or tiles that snap together without an adhesive.

Cork flooring is considered sustainable because the bark is peeled from a live tree without damage to the tree or its habitat. Cork is super quiet and resilient, and it repels mold and mildew, so can be a boon for chemically sensitive families.

Rubber can look fun or functional depending on the color and texture. Rubber is comfortable, very easy to clean, and very tough, but it can be relatively pricey compared to other resilient flooring. Rubber flooring made from recycled rubber products is relatively green.

Vinyl flooring is the least expensive of the resilient flooring materials, but it's not the shiny no-wax flooring that it once was. It's usually made of a tough outer coating, a clear vinyl layer, a printed layer of any design or color (like laminate flooring), and a bottom layer of felt or fiberglass. Vinyl is available in large sheets or tiles, with sheets providing more water resistance because there are fewer vulnerable seams.

Linoleum flooring is considered more green than most flooring because it's fairly easy to manufacture and its ingredients are naturally available: linseed oil, wood flour, limestone, tree resins, and jute. Request a solvent-free adhesive and you've got one of the greenest flooring materials around, as linoleum is completely biodegradable or recyclable. Like other resilient floorings, linoleum is soft underfoot and easy to install. Unlike vinyl, it's homogenous throughout.

more about...
LAMINATES

laminate flooring is similar to a plastic-laminate countertop in that a clear wear layer protects a photo layer that looks like wood, tile, or stone or is simply a pattern or solid color. These two layers are laminated to a high-density fiberboard and a moisture-resistant Melamine bottom layer. Today's laminate flooring planks or tiles float on a smooth underlayment (cork is a quiet and economical choice for underlayment) and usually fit together tightly without glue. Laminate flooring is relatively economical, easy to install, comfortable to stand on, and easy to clean, but the joints aren't impervious to puddled water. Window shop online but look and touch real laminate samples; you will be surprised at how much they look like the real thing. For more realistic wood-like flooring, look for surface embossing that matches the texture you see in the photo layer.

ABOVE This slender urban kitchen is finished with a running bond stone tile floor. The stone is well sealed for shine and resistance to staining.

BELOW This kitchen's three big surfaces—white painted walls and ceiling and pale limestone floor—create a backdrop that allows the red, black, and stainless steel to stand out.

ABOVE This ceramic tile makes a durable, stylish floor, and gives much more bang for the buck than stone tile. An elegant crown molding makes a smooth transition between cabinets and ceiling.

ceramic and stone tile have been classic flooring materials for several millennia for the same reason we love them today: They can be elegant, extremely durable, and will last a very, very long time. Ceramic tile has a glazed layer over a white body. Porcelain, quarry, brick, and stone tiles have color through the body, so chips won't be as apparent. Any stone can be made into tiles, with marble, limestone, granite, and slate being the most common.

All stone tiles, except for soapstone, require regular sealing to resist staining, as do unglazed tiles. An alternative to stone tile, which can be very expensive, is glazed ceramic tile that looks like stone. Glazed ceramic tile has the advantage of being waterproof and stainproof. Joints between tiles of any type are vulnerable and may require sealing. The narrower the joint and the bigger the tile, the less to seal, of course. The downside to stone and ceramic tile flooring is its otherwise praised durability: It's hard on your feet and your back and on dropped dishes. You might want to consider placing a non-slip, easy-to-clean area rug by the sink and next to your favorite prep area.

LEFT White running bond tile is the finish theme here, with large nonslip tile on the floor and smaller, subway-size tile on the backsplash. Both surfaces create a bright backdrop for warm wood cabinets and dark soapstone countertops.

ABOVE AND FACING PAGE, BOTTOM Concrete can make beautiful and exotic kitchen floors. These have a mix of aggregate colors for extra color and texture. The control joints direct cracking, a normal process for large expanses of concrete.

RIGHT This kitchen/living room is housed in what will someday be the garage, once the home is built a few years from now. The floor is finely finished concrete, which makes a great floor for either use.

more about...
CONCRETE

concrete can be stunningly beautiful as a floor material, but it requires great skill to design, place, finish, and seal properly, so it's critical to find a reputable craftsman or study proper procedures well if doing it yourself. Concrete is very hard and durable but it will develop cracks, so joints should be cut or cast where recommended; make these part of the design rather than an afterthought. And concrete will stain, so it must be sealed. Concrete can take on any color and design. It can be colored throughout the mix, or color can be added after it's placed with powder or liquid. Concrete is ideal over a radiant-heat system.

walls and ceilings

●●● MATERIALS AND FINISHES FOR CEILINGS and for walls without cabinets may be able to take a backseat until cabinets, countertops, and flooring are selected, but you can strengthen your overall design scheme by choosing these surfaces early. Of course, wall and ceiling configurations requiring structural attention must be designed from the beginning of a kitchen project, and a kitchen's lighting scheme should go hand in hand with the ceiling design and even with wall surfaces, as you may want to consider accent lighting for artwork. But you can play around with wall finishes in particular, as they are relatively easy to change. And thank goodness because painting or wall-papering walls can be an economical and speedy way to update a tired kitchen.

Think of walls in horizontal segments, with lower sections being prone to dents and splatters. Wood paneling, washable wallpaper, and glossy or semigloss paints are perfect for these more vulnerable areas. Patterns and textures can hide scuffs and scrapes. Upper walls are ideal for lighter colors, wallpaper, or artwork that will maintain an airy feel in the kitchen. The very top of a wall is ideal for trim or for a wallpaper or painted frieze.

The typical kitchen ceiling is flat and dotted with recessed can lights. While this might be what a busy kitchen needs, try to think outside that box. For higher ceilings, consider ringing the kitchen with a cove housing recessed lights, or finish a high room with a paneled barrel vault. A ceiling change over one part of the kitchen creates a design focus. Color can transform a kitchen ceiling. A dark ceiling adds coziness, whereas a light ceiling adds height. Lighting the ceiling is important because it simulates the bright outdoor sky and will cheer you up on a winter day.

There's nothing shy and unassuming about this ceiling, with its dark-stained paneling, skylight, and long row of light pendants.

ABOVE Every surface in this big New England kitchen has received detailed attention, from the cool green-gray beadboard ceiling to the expanses of tile backsplash and elegant ceramic tile floor.

ABOVE Chalkboard paint makes a wall both practical and fun, perfect for a giant shopping list or weekly schedule, or as a surface for drawing.

ABOVE Turning these large black-and-white tiles diagonally really livens up the kitchen. Crossed battens on the fridge paneling and occasional cabinets repeat the diagonal scheme.

LEFT Lowering the ceiling of this kitchen redo, then finishing it off with deep beams reinforced the shape and presence of the kitchen proper.

FACING PAGE This glass-and-steel grid is both a floor for the living space above and a decorative ceiling for the kitchen. The dark tile floor grounds the space.

LEFT A giant wood pegboard at the edge of the kitchen adds texture and utility, and the tangerine orange hallway beyond adds color from a distance. Another wall treatment is the bank of windows, so the changing seasons provide a backdrop.

ABOVE A lowered mahogany ceiling indicates the dividing line between kitchen and dining/bar areas in this kitchen addition.

ABOVE Wood beadboard with decorative beams creates a lively ceiling for a modest-size kitchen. The dark tone is repeated on the wood floor. A glass tile backsplash picks up whites, tones of stainless steel, and a bit of the reddish brown to match the ceiling and floor.

windows and lighting

9

● ● ●

A WELL-LIT KITCHEN BRIGHTENS YOUR LIFE BOTH DAY AND NIGHT, while a dimly lit kitchen will make you want to eat out even for breakfast. Make sure your kitchen is of the well-lit variety by supplying light from several types of fixtures and from several directions. Natural light from windows is primary in the daytime. Supplement that light for close work on interior countertops, and at night look to a combination of low and high fixtures that will provide both ambient and task lighting, the two most important lighting types. You may want to add the two secondary types of lighting—accent and decorative—for style and atmosphere. Provide dimmable lighting if you can, and switch the various sources of light separately to suit a variety of moods and situations as well as to save on energy use. Chandeliers and pendant lights can be expensive, but in general, electrical fixtures and wiring require a relatively small percentage of the overall design and construction budget if lighting is controlled properly. The thoughtful use of natural lighting can lower your electrical bill, and so can the proper placement and use of energy-efficient fixtures and bulbs.

Decorative objects don't get dusty as fast behind closed doors, so you won't regret fitting up a few wall cabinets with glass-panel doors. And why not add lighting to the sides or top of the cabinet, and set up the cabinet with glass shelves.

windows

● ● ● UNLESS THE WESTERN SUN IS GLARING IN your eyes as you make dinner, there's probably no amount of daylight that's too much for a kitchen. Ample windows sub for artificial lighting and provide heat gain when you want it; use overhangs, shades, and curtains to moderate the heat gain when you don't want it. In temperate weather, open windows can provide makeup air to balance the exhaust from a powerful range hood.

Locate windows high enough to bounce light off the ceiling or position them close to countertop level for task lighting, or make them tall enough for both tasks. Consider forgoing wall cabinets on exterior walls in favor of windows. You'll gain a lovely view or even just the ability to look beyond the kitchen into the backyard or a driveway; an extended view relieves your eyes and increases the perceived size of the kitchen. If you really need those wall cabinets, consider adding skylights to boost brightness without taking up wall space. A deep well creates a more diffuse light and can reduce glaring sunlight. Powered shades can prevent midday glare.

ABOVE Square skylights are glazed with frosted glass to reduce glare and to let in a soft light that illuminates not only the island but the perimeter countertops. Undercabinet lights, cable-mounted fixtures, and recessed downlights make up the difference on cloudy days and, of course, at night.

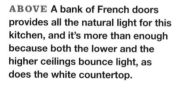

ABOVE A bank of French doors provides all the natural light for this kitchen, and it's more than enough because both the lower and the higher ceilings bounce light, as does the white countertop.

FACING PAGE A modest-size, high-style contemporary kitchen receives its natural light via glazed French doors and sidelights. White flip-door cabinets and countertops and stainless steel help bounce light around. Undercabinet fixtures, pendants, and downlights provide artificial lighting.

RIGHT These clerestory windows—so-called because they are above the level of a standard room height—allow daylight to bounce off the ceiling to create a diffuse, ambient glow.

A high-style pendant supplies task and ambient light to the dining end of a big kitchen island. In-cabinet light fixtures add sparkle.

lighting

● ● ● EACH TYPE OF LIGHTING HAS ITS OWN function in a kitchen. **Ambient lighting** brightens the whole room to a certain extent, prevents harsh shadows, and makes it easy to move around. In the daytime, natural light can provide most of the ambient light a kitchen needs, while at night, ambient light is handled by pendants or chandeliers, recessed lights, track lights, and concealed above-cabinet fixtures.

Task lighting illuminates where you work, whether it's a countertop, cooktop, or sink, and whether on an island or at a desk. Task lighting should be natural in color and bright enough to work easily. Undercabinet fixtures of all shapes and sizes can provide task lighting, as can pendants, track lights, and recessed can lights. Task lights positioned close to the workspace are more efficient than lights positioned on the ceiling.

Accent lighting illuminates specific objects such as dishware or art objects, or it can wash a wall. Recessed fixtures that can be focused, track lighting, in-cabinet fixtures, and sconces can all act as accent lights. Decorative lighting is itself a source of beauty—think chandeliers and pendants—but it can also provide task, ambient, or accent lighting.

ⓖⓐⓛⓛⓔⓡⓨ

pendants and chandeliers

Pendants and chandeliers can add style to a kitchen, but they can also boost ambient and task lighting. Pendants are perfect for lighting an island, and they are perfect for dining surfaces. But pendants can work well for lighting other work areas, too, because they bring the light source closer to the workspace. Choose pendants that are fairly easy to clean, and consider height, spacing, and how the light appears to a seated cook or diner. As a rule, hang a pendant 30 in. above dining and 36 in. above a work surface—even higher for tall ceilings or wide fixtures. Prevent glare by choosing a fixture with a shielded or frosted bulb. Choose a semi-opaque, translucent, or transparent shade to allow more ambient light to reach the ceiling.

ABOVE Blown-glass pendants provide stylish task and ambient lighting to the island in a small kitchen. Square downlights and round puck lights add ambient and task lighting to the perimeter. The center cabinet conceals a narrow refrigerator/freezer.

ABOVE Not only do these handsome pendants light the workspace but their large translucent shades help illuminate the ceiling.

LEFT Two styles of pendants serve different functions in this tall kitchen/dining space. The large decorative pendant provides light for dining, and the more delicate pendants add both ambient and island task lighting.

gallery

recessed, surface-mounted, and track lighting

Recessed downlights are all over kitchens and have been for decades, but do consider other types of lighting fixtures, either as better suited to the job or as supplemental lighting. Adjustable recessed downlights provide drama and make ideal accent lights for art and decorative dishware, but drama may not be needed for lighting kitchen workspaces. Downlights can't light a ceiling well, which limits their use for ambient lighting. Task lighting is most efficient when the light source is close to the surface it is lighting. A ceiling downlight is relatively far from a workspace, so its bulb must be considerably brighter to produce the light required for safe and comfortable work, which reduces overall energy efficiency. Still, recessed downlights are popular and easy to purchase in many sizes, shapes, trim colors, reflector colors and sizes, baffle configurations, and bulb types. Space downlights close enough to allow light pools to overlap on the countertop or floor. Avoid downlights that allow air and moisture to leak into the ceiling cavity or an attic space. Downlights labeled IC-A have airtight housing and can be tightly wrapped with insulation.

Surface-mounted fixtures, also called flush mounted or ceiling mounted, can provide ambient, task, and accent lighting and can themselves be decorative lights. Surface-mounted lights with translucent or transparent shades or lenses allow light to shine upward to the ceiling and bounce back into the kitchen, improving ambience and safety. Track lighting comes in all shapes and sizes, and includes high- and low-voltage systems with pendants and adjustable spots. Track lights are not only individually adjustable—giving them the drama of recessed downlights and the flexibility to light the ceiling—but can offer the full range of lighting functions from ambient to decorative. One type of track lighting is the flexible rail fixture, which can be shaped to provide decorative, accent, and even task lighting.

ABOVE Cantilevered shelves line up against the backsplash as both storage and to provide concealed space for recessed puck task lighting. Glossy penny mosaic tiles help bounce light without harsh reflections.

ABOVE Clerestory windows brighten a kitchen without adding glare to workspaces. Cable fixtures add ambient light at night and on cloudy days and create patterns on beams.

LEFT Downlights can be strictly utilitarian, but they also can become a design feature, as in this well-lit kitchen, with perimeter downlights at the ceiling and directional downlights creating a pattern on the hood.

FACING PAGE, RIGHT Several sources of lighting serve this small kitchen. Recessed puck fixtures light the sink, undercabinet fixtures light all countertops, and hood fixtures light the countertop. Downlights supply ambient light at night.

LIGHTING CONTROLS AND RECEPTACLES

Y ou'll be happiest with your kitchen lighting if you can adjust lights individually and in groups, and with ease. Automated control systems allow you, or your lighting designer, to program in many lighting scenarios that you can call up by touching a pad. These systems can be hugely convenient, but they're also complex and expensive. Wireless versions are available for a higher price. A more economical alternative is to install rotary, slide, or touch dimmer controls, and provide switches and dimmers at main entry points. Cluster switches for convenience; stack multiple switches if that looks better to your eye than lining them up.

Receptacles—we also call them outlets—don't have to be a necessary evil in kitchen design. Consider ways to have them blend in or just think of them as a design element. If you're in the blending-in camp, tuck plug molding, a continuous strip of outlets, under a wall cabinet or along the backsplash. Although plug molding keeps the backsplash clear of receptacles and offers many outlets, be aware that appliance cords will be visible when the appliance is plugged in. For receptacles in a backsplash, you'll want to consider location and color more carefully. Receptacle plates can act as color accents or can be camouflaged with faux painting or matching wallpaper. For a tile backsplash, coordinate receptacle location with the tile layout. Fixed islands will require receptacles, too, but these are harder to disguise. A two-height island offers a perfect backsplash location for island receptacles. A hollowed island leg can make a good home for a receptacle, too. Minimize a receptacle's presence by selecting small, round receptacle plates that match the color of the surroundings. Cover low receptacles as an even better disguise, and for safety.

ABOVE Receptacles are required at a certain spacing in a kitchen, but they don't have to be set into a lovely tile backsplash if there's another alternative, like this single sill-mounted receptacle with a cover.

LEFT White downlights create a subtle visual presence but have a big impact on ambient and task lighting. The clear glass shades on the island pendants allow light to bounce off the ceiling.

LEFT In this Oregon kitchen, three types of ceiling-mounted fixtures repeat the light–dark tone scheme. The small ceiling-mounted fixtures are a traditional alternative to downlights. Concealed undercabinet fixtures supply task lighting.

m o r e   a b o u t . . .

LIGHTBULBS

lightbulbs sure aren't what they used to be, thanks to efforts to improve energy efficiency and longevity. (The lighting industry calls bulbs *lamps,* but the term *bulb* will do here.) Incandescent bulbs, which contain filaments, include tungsten (the standard lightbulb) and halogen, which is more energy efficient and long-lived than tungsten. Incandescent lights are extremely inefficient because only 10% of the energy used by the bulb produces light and the excess escapes as heat; hence they are slowly being phased out of production.

Compact fluorescent lamps (CFLs) can fit into standard lamp bases and cost more than incandescent bulbs but use about 75% less energy and last about 10 times as long. CFL color rendition has greatly improved; choose bulbs with a color temperature of 2,700 to 3,000 Kelvin for the warmest,

most incandescent-like color (the higher the Kelvin rating, the more like daylight, which is actually much cooler in tone than incandescent lighting). Or look for a color-rendering index (CRI) of 80 or higher for a warmer tone. It's true that CFLs contain a minute amount of mercury, and this needs to be carefully cleaned up if a lamp is broken. But the use of CFLs instead of incandescents reduces the overall amount of mercury emissions from power plants by a significant amount, far outweighing the mercury that ends up in a landfill from worn-out or broken CFLs. Light-emitting diode (LED) fixtures are extremely long lasting and pleasing in color, and can be somewhat more energy efficient than CFLs. LEDs remain very expensive, but are becoming somewhat more affordable.

•lighting wall cabinets inside and below

Undercabinet fixtures can provide ideal task lighting for working countertops because the light source is close to the surface (therefore more energy efficient), and it's easy to conceal behind the cabinet case or door. But undercabinet lights can provide ambient light, too, especially if the backsplash and countertop are light in tone and softly reflective. Note that undercabinet lights will be reflected more clearly in a polished countertop; select a honed, brushed, or matte countertop and backsplash for a softer reflected light. To avoid glare and harsh reflections, install undercabinet fixtures along the bottom front inside edge of wall cabinets.

Halogen undercabinet puck lights are bright white and easy to install, but they generate a lot of heat. Shallow fluorescent tubes are very long-lasting, energy-efficient, and inexpensive. Xenon tubes are cooler running and longer-lived than halogen and have a warmer tint than some fluorescent tubes. Small LED (light-emitting diode) undercabinet fixtures are extremely long lasting and quite energy efficient but very expensive. These same fixture types can add ambience and spaciousness to a kitchen when added above wall cabinets, where they can light the ceiling.

Light the interiors of glass-door wall cabinets for ambience and accent lighting. Glass shelves add extra mileage to in-cabinet light fixtures. Pantries are ideal for door-operated task lighting.

These undercabinet puck lights can't be seen by the cook, but they provide welcome task lighting to a textured black granite countertop. The white glass backsplash helps reflect light, too.

BELOW This two-level backsplash creates a space for concealed compact-fluorescent tube lighting and for attaching shelving.

ABOVE Recessed puck lights alone provide plenty of task illumination for washing up, but the glass mosaic tile gives a reflective boost, as does the marble countertop.

ABOVE Twin-strip LED fixtures provide subtle and good-looking task lighting for a serving cabinet. The Olympian Silver marble and glass-tile backsplash help reflect and bounce light. A subtle plug molding trims the back under the cabinets.

LEFT Recessed undercabinet lights provide task lighting under all wall cabinets, and occasional lengths of plug molding offer many outlets for appliances. The plug molding can't be seen by a standing cook.

FACING PAGE Undercabinet lighting provides a bright kitchen with task lighting, while pendants and downlights supply both ambient and task lighting.

resources

You could research kitchen ideas 24/7 if you had that kind of time, but who does? Instead, focus on these: information from industry experts and manufacturers, advice from users, visual inspiration, and comparison shopping. For inspiration and advice, look to books and magazines both for skimming and studying in detail. The most useful kitchen books and magazines are more than just a corkboard for pretty pictures—they're sources of information about materials and methods. And because book and magazine publishers look for new content, you will likely find photos of kitchens you've not already seen all over the Internet.

Use the Internet to get inspiration, learn about new products, compare product costs, and read user advice. Maintain a skeptical eye as you read the myriad opinions on everything under the sun; among the many valid reviews are write-ups that are actually product placements (or bashing). And while you'll want to do preliminary shopping online, verify in person, if you can. Check out appliances, cabinets, sinks and fittings, flooring, and hardware in showrooms and shops.

In this section are resources I've found to be helpful but that you may not have tapped yet.

You may find that an organization's or company's Web site is less up to date than their Facebook[SM] or Twitter[SM] account; other organizations have a light social media presence.

INFORMATION ABOUT DESIGN AND ENERGY

aarp.org
This is the AARP Web site. Search for "kitchen design" to find tips for making any kitchen more accessible.

ap.buffalo.edu/idea/home
This is the Web site of the Center for Inclusive Design and Environmental Access at the State University of New York at Buffalo. It's a comprehensive source for universal design concepts and education.

energystar.gov
Energy Star is a joint program of the U.S. Environmental Protection Agency and the U.S. Department of Energy with the stated goals of saving money and protecting the environment through energy efficient products and practices. This good-looking, easy-to-navigate Web site is packed with information on how to build and live more efficiently. The program reviews and rates appliances and whole houses, giving the best performing the designation of Energy Star. Also look here for information about compact fluorescent lightbulbs and other energy-saving devices.

fsc.org
Per the Forest Stewardship Council Web site, "FSC certification is a voluntary, market-based tool that supports responsible forest management worldwide. FSC certified forest products are verified from the forest of origin through the supply chain. The FSC label ensures that the forest products used are from responsibly harvested and verified sources." Seek out FSC-certified woods for a more sustainable kitchen.

greenbuildingadvisor.com
Green Building Advisor (GBA) is a Taunton Press Web site that draws on the family-owned company's decades of publishing information about building houses. Its large pool of editors includes current or former builders, remodelers, designers, engineers, and other experts in the field of homebuilding. The site offers construction drawings, detailed advice, a green products database, and green building business strategies. Comments on articles are intelligent, conversational, and to the point, unlike most Web commentary, and there is plenty of lively but civil argument. Much of GBA's information is free, including an email newsletter and downloads of white-paper information about topics like lead abatement and how to maintain a green building business. Full access to GBA's deep reservoir of expertise and product reviews is available by subscription monthly or yearly.

nkba.org
From the National Kitchen & Bath Association: "The National Kitchen & Bath Association (NKBA) is a leading nonprofit trade association dedicated to the advancement of the kitchen & bath industry." Its Web site offers information primarily for design professionals but also provides consumers with design advice. Its illustrated NKBA Kitchen & Bath Planning Guidelines with Access Standards is a useful document for laying out kitchens, with or without universal design in mind.

The Taunton Press
The Taunton Press's publications and Web sites offer the most in-depth information you can find about the construction and design of homes. Visit taunton.com/books and click on "Home Design" to find design and how-to books for kitchens and kitchen elements. Pick up any issue of Fine Homebuilding to find at least one house design article, and don't pass up any of the annual Kitchens and Baths issues and the annual Houses issue. Both cover design and materials in great depth. Fine Homebuilding offers some articles for free on its Web site (www.finehomebuilding.com), plus other free Web extras like how-to videos, blogs, and resource lists. For me, and for anyone who loves digging deeply into home design, the yearly or monthly fee to access all the magazine's content is well spent.

BOOKS

Jordan, Wendy A. Universal Design for the Home. Minneapolis, MN: Quarry Books, 2008.
Universal design—design that allows people of all abilities to live comfortably and productively—is of increasing interest to designers and homeowners, especially as baby boomers start to retire. This book contains much helpful information about kitchens.

McAlester, Virginia, and Lee McAlester. A Field Guide to American Houses. New York: Alfred Knopf, 1984.
I'm sure this 28-year-old book remains in print because it's still the best guide about American house style. Look especially at the many drawings of wood trim profiles and windows, noting proportions, and operation type.

Roberts, Jennifer. Good Green Kitchens. Layton, UT: Gibbs Smith, 2006.
The LEED[SM] (Leadership in Energy and Environmental Design)-accredited author offers detailed suggestions for designing and building a green kitchen.

designers

The following designers and architects have multiple photos or projects in this book.

Albertsson Hansen Architecture
Minneapolis, MN
aharchitecture.com

Alexandra Immel Design
Seattle, WA
Alexandraimmeldesign.com

Arkin Tilt Architects
Berkeley, CA
arkintilt.com

Bay Point Builders
Newton, MA
baypointbuilderscorp.com

Bonaventura Architects
Brooklyn, NY
bonaventuraarchitect.com

Butz + Klug Architects
Boston, MA
bkarch.com

CAST Architecture
Seattle, WA
castarchitecture.com

Christine Tuttle Interior Design
Wellesley, MA
christinetuttle.com

Conner & Buck Builders, Ltd.
Bristol, VT
connerandbuck.com

Cushman Design Group
Stowe, VT
cushmandesign.com

CWB Architects
Brooklyn, NY
cwbarchitects.com

Daher Interior Design
Boston, MA
daherinteriordesign.com

David Heide Design Studio
Minneapolis, MN
dhdstudio.com

Paul DeGroot
Austin, TX
degrootarchitect.com

Eck/MacNeely Architects Inc.
Boston, MA
eckmacneely.com

George Gekas Design
Bass Harbor, ME
georgegekasdesign.com

Reid Highley
Chapel Hill, NC
highleyarchitect.com

Hutker Architects
Falmouth, MA
hutkerarchitects.com

Andrew Jacobson
Petaluma, CA
designinwoodinc.com

Jennifer Baines Interiors
Lake Oswego, OR
jennybaines.com

Jessica Helgerson Interior Design
Portland, OR
jhinteriordesign.com

Caleb Johnson
Biddeford, ME
calebjohnsonarchitects.com

Laura Kaehler Architects
Greenwich, CT
kaehlerarchitects.com

Daniel Meyers
Olympia, WA
meyerswoodworks.com

Dave Mulder
Grand Rapids, MI
fourbyeight.com

Ogawa Fisher Architects
Portland, OR
ogawafisher.com

Pamela Copeman Design Group
Nantasket Beach, MA
pamelacopeman.com

Phi Home Designs
Camden, ME
phihomedesigns.com

Polhemus Savery DaSilva Architects/ Builders
Chatham, MA
psdab.com

Poteet Architects
San Antonio, TX
poteetarchitects.com

Rehkamp Larson Architects
Minneapolis, MN
rehkamplarson.com

Robin Colton of Laura Britt Design
Austin, TX
laurabrittdesign.com

Ruhl Walker Architects
Boston, MA
ruhlwalker.com

South Mountain Company
West Tisbury MA
southmountain.com

Treehouse Design
Rockport, MA
treehousedesigninc.com

Zero Energy Design
Boston, MA
zeroenergy.com

photo credits

CHAPTER 1

p. 4: Photo © Lincoln Barbour, Design: Jessica Helgerson Interior Design

p. 6: Photo © Eric Roth, Design: Butz + Klug Architects

p. 7: (left) Photo © Susan Gilmore, Design: David Heide Design Studio; (top right) Photo © Ryann Ford, Design: Kimberly Renner of The Renner Project with Kim Coffin, Austin, TX; (bottom right) Photo © Eric Roth

p. 8: Photo © Adan Torres, Design: Rehkamp Larson Architects; Woodworks Cabinetry, Keith Johnson

p. 9: (top right) Photo © Hulya Kolabas, Design: Laura Kaehler Architects; (bottom) Photo © Adan Torres, Design: Albertsson Hansen Architects

p. 10: (top) Photo © Eric Roth, Design: Siemasko Verbridge, Beverly, MA; (bottom) Photo © Hulya Kolabas, Design: Laura Kaehler Architects

p. 11: Photo © Lincoln Barbour, Design: Jessica Helgerson

p. 12: Photo © Susan Gilmore, Design: David Heide Design Studio

p. 13: (left) Photo © Sozinho Imagery, Design: CAST Architecture; (right) Photo © Mark Lohman

p. 14: Photo © Eric Roth, Design: SpaceCraft Architecture, Lexington, MA

p. 15: (top) Photo © Hulya Kolabas, Design: CWB Architects; (bottom left) Photo © Brian Vanden Brink, Design: Polhemus Savery DaSilva Architects Builders; (bottom right) Photo © Eric Roth, Design: Butz + Klug Architects

p. 16: (both) Photos © Hulya Kolabas, Design: Laura Kaehler Architects

p. 17: (left) Photo © Hulya Kolabas, Design: Laura Kaehler Architects; (right) Photo © Trent Bell, Design: Robson Bilgen Architects, Hancock, VT

p. 18: Photo © Adan Torres, Design: Rehkamp Larson Architects

p. 19: (left) Photo © Brian Vanden Brink, Design: Blas Bruno, Architect, Blue Hill, ME; (right) Photo © Trent Bell, Design: Caleb Johnson Architects

p. 20: (top) Photo © Susan Gilmore, Design: David Heide Design Studio; (bottom) Photo © Hulya Kolabas

p. 21: Photo © Hulya Kolabas, Design: Bonaventura Architects

p. 22: (left) Photo © Hulya Kolabas, Design: CWB Architects; (right) Photo © Ryann Ford, Design: Poteet Architects

p. 23: Photo © Brian Vanden Brink, Design: Phi Home Designs

p. 24: Photo © Lincoln Barbour, Design: Kenton McSween, Portland, OR

p. 25: (left) Photo © Hulya Kolabas, Design: Jeff Kaufman of JMKA Architects & Christopher Peacock Home, Greenwich, CT; (right) Photo © Brian Vanden Brink, Design: Phi Home Designs

p. 26: Photo © Trent Bell, Design: Van Dam Architecture & Design, Portland, ME

p. 27: (top) Photo © Eric Roth, Design: Centerbrook Architects & Tracy Harris Designs, Centerbrook, CT; (bottom) Photo © Brian Vanden Brink, Design: Hutker Architects

p. 28: (top) Photo © Eric Roth ; (bottom) Photo © Eric Roth, Design: Howell Custom Building Group, Lawrence, MA

p. 29: (top) Photo © Eric Roth, Design: Timothy Burke Architecture, Boston, MA; Builder: Woodbourne Builders Inc., Westwood, MA; (bottom) Photo © Mark Lohman

p. 30: Photo © Eric Roth, Design: Jeff Swanson, Renovation Planning, Boston, MA

p. 31: (both) Photos © Adan Torres, Design: Albertsson Hansen Architects

p. 32: Photo © Eric Roth, Design: Ruhl Walker Architects

p. 33: (top) Photo Rob Yagid © The Taunton Press, Design: CAST Architecture; (bottom left) Photo Charles Bickford © The Taunton Press, Design: Dave Mulder, fourbyeight.com, Grand Rapids, MI; (bottom right) Photo © Sozinho Imagery, Design: CAST Architecture

p. 34: (top left) Photo © Hulya Kolabas, Design: Laura Kaehler Architects; (top right) Photo Charles Miller © The Taunton Press, Design: Robin Colton of Laura Britt Design; (bottom) Photo © Eric Roth, Design: John Day at Hutker Architects

p. 35: (bottom) Photo © Sozinho Imagery, Design: CAST Architecture

p. 36: (top) Photo © Hulya Kolabas, Design: Bonaventura Architects; (bottom) Photo © Sozinho Imagery, Design: HyBrid Architecture, Seattle, WA

p. 37: (top) Photo © Adan Torres, Design: Albertsson Hansen Architects; (middle) Photo © Lincoln Barbour, Design: Ogawa Fisher Architects; (bottom) Photo © Hulya Kolabas, Design: Laura Kaehler Architects

CHAPTER 2

p. 38: Photo © Eric Roth

p. 40: Photo © Ryann Ford, Design: Poteet Architects

p. 41: (top) Photo © Hulya Kolabas, Design: Laura Kaehler Architects; (bottom) Photo © Eric Roth

p. 42: (top and bottom right) Photos © Lincoln Barbour, Design: Jessica Helgerson Interior Design; (bottom left) Photo © Sozinho Imagery, Design: CAST Architecture

p. 44: Photo © Greg Premru, Design: Zero Energy Design

p. 45: (top) Photo © Brian Vanden Brink, Design: Eric A Chase Architecture, South Brooksville, ME; (bottom) Photo © Eric Roth, Design: Siemasko Verbridge, Beverly, MA

p. 46: Photo © Susan Teare, Design: Cushman Design Group

p. 47: (top) Photo © Eric Roth, Design: Scandia Kitchens, Bellingham, MA; (bottom left) Photo © Ken Gutmaker, Design: Rehkamp Larson Architects; (bottom right) Photo © Hulya Kolabas, Design: Laura Kaehler Architects

p. 48: Photo © Eric Roth, Design: Christine Tuttle Interior; Breese Architects, Vineyard Haven, MA; Cabinets: Balthaup

p. 49: (top left) Photo © Hulya Kolabas, Design: Bonaventura Architects; (top right) Photo Brian Pontolilo © The Taunton Press, Design: Eugene Wilson Brown, NC, Raleigh; (bottom) Photo © Joanne Bouknight, Design: Laura Kaehler Architects

p. 50: Photo © Ryann Ford, Design: Anabel Interiors, Austin, TX

p. 51: (top) Photo © Sozinho Imagery, Design: CAST Architecture; (bottom left) Photo Rob Yagid © The Taunton Press, Design: Tina Govan, Architect, Raleigh, NC; (bottom right) Photo © Hulya Kolabas, Design: Laura Kaehler Architects

CHAPTER 3

p. 52: Photo © Lincoln Barbour, Design: Jessica Helgerson Interior Design

p. 54: Photo © Eric Roth, Design: Hutker Architects, Falmouth, MA

p. 55: (top left) Photo © Hulya Kolabas, Design: Laura Kaehler Architects; (top right) Photo © Brian Vanden Brink, Design: Albert, Righter and Tittman Architects, Boston, MA; (bottom) Photo © Hulya Kolabas, Design: Laura Kaehler Architects

p. 56: Photo Charles Miller © The Taunton Press, Design: Arkin Tilt Architects

p. 57: (top) Photo © Sozinho Imagery, Design: CAST Architecture; (bottom) Photo © Kevin Casey, Design: Alexandra Immel Design

p. 58: (left) Photo Charles Bickford © The Taunton Press, Design: Dave Mulder, fourbyeight.com; (right) Photo © Adan Torres, Design: Rehkamp Larson Architects

p. 59: Photo © Susan Gilmore, Design: Rehkamp Larson Architects

p. 60: (left) Photo © Trent Bell, Design: Charles R. Myer & Partners, Ltd., Cambridge, MA and Taylor Interior Design, Providence, RI; (right) Photo © Hulya Kolabas, Design: Bonaventura Architects

p. 61: (left) Photo © Greg Premru, Design: Moger Mehrhof Architects, Annapolis, MD; (right) Photo Charles Miller © The Taunton Press, Design: Ty Allen, RA, Maxine Bromfield, Jonathan Orphin, Portland, OR

p. 62: (left) Photo © Ross Anania, Design: Alexandra Immel Design; (right) Photo © Rau + Barber, Design: Rehkamp Larson Architects

p. 63: Photo © Hulya Kolabas, Design: Bonaventura Architects

p. 64: (top) Photo © Eric Roth, Design: Paine Bouchier, Boston, MA; (bottom) Photo © Eric Roth, Design: Ruhl Walker Architects

p. 66: (top) Photo Charles Miller © The Taunton Press, Design: JSWD Architects: Helen Degenhardt, principal architect, with Max Jacobson, Berkeley, CA; (bottom left) Photo © Susan Gilmore, Design: Rehkamp Larson Architects; (bottom right) Photo © Eric Roth, Design: Bay Point Builders

p. 67: Photo © Hulya Kolabas, Design: CWB Architects

p. 68: (both top) Photos © Hulya Kolabas, Design: Laura Kaehler Architects; (bottom) Photo © Ken Gutmaker, Design: Rehkamp Larson Architects

p. 69: Photo © Lincoln Barbour, Design: Ogawa Fisher Architects

p. 70: Photo © Hulya Kolabas, Design: Laura Kaehler Architects

p. 71: (top) Photo © Eric Roth, Design: Boardman Design, Cambridge, MA; (bottom) Photo © Eric Roth

p. 72: (both) Photos © Hulya Kolabas, Design: Laura Kaehler Architects

p. 73: (left) Photo © Brian Vanden Brink, Design: Polhemus Savery DaSilva Architects Builders; (right) Photo © Adan Torres, Design: Rehkamp Larson Architects

CHAPTER 4

p. 74: Photo © Hulya Kolabas, Design: Laura Kaehler Architects

p. 76: Photo Charles Miller © The Taunton Press, Design: JSWD Architects: Helen Degenhardt, with Max Jacobson, Berkeley, CA

p. 77: Photo © Adan Torres, Design: Albertsson Hansen Architects

p. 78: (left) Photo © Eric Roth, Design: Horst Buchanan Architects, Inc., Jamaica Plain, MA; (right) Photo © Adan Torres, Design: Albertsson Hansen Architects

p. 79: Photo Charles Miller © The Taunton Press, Design: Cabinetmaker, Andrew Jacobson

p. 80: (top) Photo Charles Bickford © The Taunton Press, Design: Dave Mulder, fourbyeight.com; (bottom) Photo © Hulya Kolabas, Design: Laura Kaehler Architects

p. 81: Photo © Hulya Kolabas, Design: Laura Kaehler Architects

p. 82: (left) Photo © Eric Roth, Design: Christine Tuttle Interior Design; Cabinet: Bulthaup; (right) Photo © Hulya Kolabas, Design: Laura Kaehler Architects

p. 83: Photo © Eric Roth, Design: Dalia Kitchen Design, Boston, MA

p. 84: Photo © Lincoln Barbour, Design: Jessica Helgerson Interior Design

p. 85: (top) Photo © Eric Roth, Design: Eck | MacNeely Architects; (bottom) Photo Rob Yagid © The Taunton Press, Design: Nathan Good Architects, Salem, OR; David Gellos, Architect, Portland, OR

p. 86: Photo © Sozinho Imagery, Design: CAST Architecture

p. 87: (top left and bottom) Photos © Hulya Kolabas, Design: Laura Kaehler Architects; (top right) Photo © Adan Torres, Design: Rehkamp Larson Architects

p. 88: Photo © Eric Roth, Design: Dressing Rooms Interior Design, Westford, MA

p. 89: (top left) Photo © Eric Roth, Design: Pamela Copeman Design Group; (top right) Photo Charles Bickford © The Taunton Press, Design: David Getts, davidgettsdesign.com, Bothell, WA; (bottom) Photo © Sozinho Imagery, Design: CAST Architecture

p. 90: Photo © Eric Roth, Builder: Bay Point Builders

p. 91: (top) Photo Charles Bickford © The Taunton Press, Design: Cabinetmaker, Andrew Jacobson; (bottom left) Photo © Eric Roth, Design: Pamela Copeman Design Group; (bottom right) Photo © Eric Roth, Builder: Bay Point Builders

p. 92: Photo © Eric Roth, Design: Pamela Copeman Design Group

p. 93: (top) Photo © Hulya Kolabas, Design: Laura Kaehler Architects; (bottom) Photo © Ken Gutmaker, Design: Rehkamp Larson Architects

p. 94: (left) Photo Charles Miller © The Taunton Press, Design: Andrew Jacobson; (right) Photo © Hulya Kolabas, Design: Laura Kaehler Architects

p. 95: (both) Photos © Adan Torres, Design: Rehkamp Larson Architects

p. 96: Photo © Mark Lohman

p. 97: (both) Photos © Adan Torres, Design: Rehkamp Larson Architects

p. 98: Photo © Mark Lohman, Design: Taddey & Karlin, Los Angeles, CA

p. 99: (top) Photo © Eric Roth, Design: Eleven Interiors, Boston, MA; (bottom) Photo © Adan Torres, Design: Albertsson Hansen Architects

p. 100: Photo © Brian Vanden Brink, Design: Polhemus Savery DaSilva Architects Builders

p. 101: Photo © Sozinho Imagery, Design: CAST Architecture

p. 102: (top) Photo © Sozinho Imagery, Design: CAST Architecture; (bottom) Photo © Adan Torres, Design: Albertsson Hansen Architects

p. 103: Photo © Hulya Kolabas, Design: Bonaventura Architects

p. 104: Photo © Trent Bell, Design: GO Logic Homes, Belfast, ME

p. 105: Photos © Hulya Kolabas, Design: Christopher Peacock Home, Greenwich, CT; JMKA Architects, Greenwich, CT; (right) Photo © Hulya Kolabas, Design: Laura Kaehler Architects

p. 106: (left) Photo © Hulya Kolabas, Design: Laura Kaehler Architects; (right) Photo © Eric Roth, Design: The Pinehills, Plymouth, MA

p. 108: Photo Charles Miller © The Taunton Press, Design: Daniel Meyers, meyerswoodworks.com

p. 109: (top) Photo © Hulya Kolabas, Design: Laura Kaehler Architects; (bottom) Photo Charles Miller © The Taunton Press, Design: Daniel Meyers, meyerswoodworks.com

p. 110: Photo © Hulya Kolabas, Design: Laura Kaehler Architects

p. 111: (left) Photo © Hulya Kolabas, Design: Bonaventura Architects; (right) Photo © Sozinho Imagery, Design: CAST Architecture

CHAPTER 5

p. 112: Photo © Eric Roth

p. 114: Photo © Lincoln Barbour, Design: Jessica Helgerson Interior Design

p. 115: (top) Rob Yagid © The Taunton Press, Design: Reid Highley; (bottom) Photo © Sozinho Imagery, Design: CAST Architecture

p. 116: (left) Photo © Sozinho Imagery, Design: CAST Architecture; (right) Photo © Adan Torres, Design: Albertsson Hansen Architects

p. 117: (both) Photos © Adan Torres, Design: Albertsson Hansen Architects

p. 118: Photo Brian Pontolilo © The Taunton Press, Design: Paul DeGroot

p. 119: (top) Photo © Adan Torres, Design: Rehkamp Larson Architects; (bottom) Photo © Hulya Kolabas, Design: Laura Kaehler Architects

p. 120: Photo © Hulya Kolabas, Design: Laura Kaehler Architects

p. 121: (top left) Photo © Eric Roth, Design: Adams and Beasley, Inc., Boston, MA; (top right and bottom) Photos © Hulya Kolabas, Design: Laura Kaehler Architects

p. 122: (left) Charles Miller © The Taunton Press, Design: Ty Allen, RA, Maxine Bromfield, Jonathan Orphin, Portland, OR; (right) Photo © Sozinho Imagery, Design: CAST Architecture

p. 123: (left) Photo Brian Pontolilo © The Taunton Press, Design: Paul DeGroot; (right) Charles Miller © The Taunton Press, Design: CAST Architecture

p. 124: (both) Photos © Adan Torres, Design: Rehkamp Larson Architects

p. 125: Photo © Eric Roth, Design: Nicole Yee Interiors, San Francisco, CA and Kittery, ME

CHAPTER 6

p. 126: Photo © Hulya Kolabas, Design: Laura Kaehler Architects

p. 128: Photo © Eric Roth, Design: Hutker Architects

p. 129: (top) Photo © Adan Torres, Design: Albertsson Hansen Architects; (bottom) Photo © Trent Bell, Design: George Gekas Design

p. 130: (left) Photo © Lincoln Barbour, Design: Jessica Helgerson Interior Design; (right) Photo © Eric Roth, Design: Carpenter & Macneille, Essex, MA

p. 131: (top) Photo © Lincoln Barbour, Design: Jennifer Baines Interiors; (bottom) Photo © Hulya Kolabas, Design: Laura Kaehler Architects

p. 132: Photo © Hulya Kolabas, Design: Laura Kaehler Architects

p. 133: (top) Photo © Adan Torres, Design: Rehkamp Larson Architects; (bottom) Photo © Hulya Kolabas

p. 134: Photo Brian Pontolilo © The Taunton Press, Design: Eugene Wilson Brown, AIA, Raleigh, NC

p. 135: (top) Photo © Brian Vanden Brink, Design: Houses and Barns by John Libby, Freeport, ME; (bottom) Photo © Adan Torres, Design: Rehkamp Larson Architects; brackets by Bo Jacobssen/ Discount Steel and Metal, Minneapolis, MN

p. 136: Photo © Eric Roth

p. 137: Photo © Eric Roth

p. 138: Photo © Eric Roth, Design: Dressing Rooms Interior Design, Westford MA

p. 139: (top) Photo © Joanne Bouknight, Design: Laura Kaehler Architects; (bottom left) Photo © Eric Roth, Design: Mark Christofi Interiors, North Reading, MA; Architect: John Carsi, Palladian Design Studio, Fort Myers, FL; (bottom right) Photo © Sozinho Imagery, Design: CAST Architecture

p. 140: (both) Photos © Adan Torres, Design: Albertsson Hansen Architects, Minneapolis, MN

p. 141: (top left) Photo Charles Bickford © The Taunton Press, Design: Robin Colton of Laura Britt Design; shelves: builder Royce Flournoy, Texas Construction Col, Austin, TX; (top right) Photo © Lincoln Barbour, Design: Jennifer Baines Interiors; (bottom) Photo © Hulya Kolabas, Design: Laura Kaehler Architects

p. 142: (top) Photo © Eric Roth, Design: Jonathan Cutler, AIA, Brookline, MA; (bottom) Photo © Susan Teare, Design: Cushman Design Group